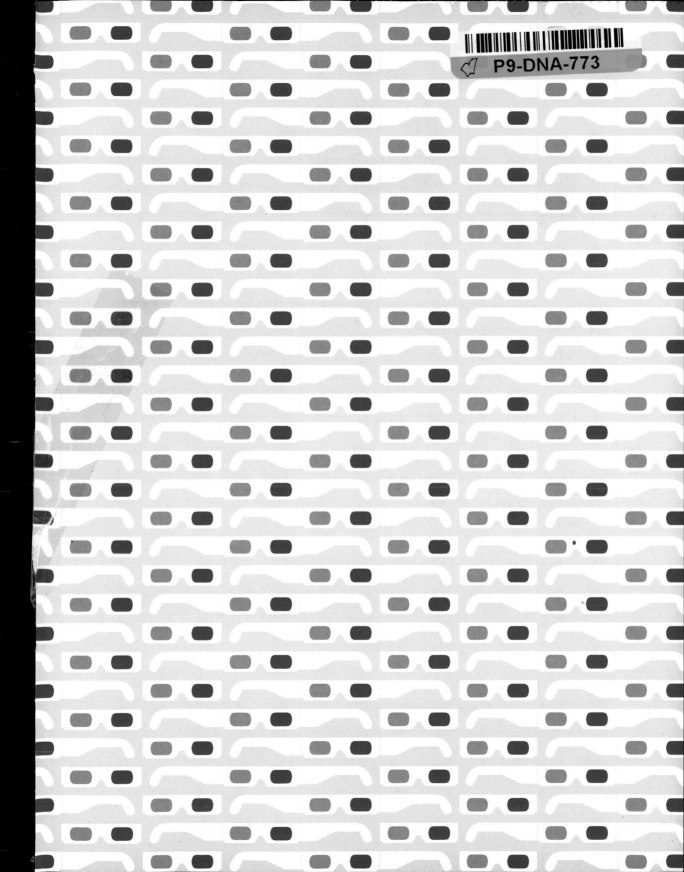

WHY THIS BOOK IS IN 3-D

EXPERIENCE DEPTHINESS!

Book Nation, my first book was a huge hit, so I could have written the exact same book again and just "rearranged the words a bit" (Ex: "bit the words a drear anger"). But I wanted this book to be bigger and better and bigter by doing all the important things to make books good, like adding full color, upgrading the photos to HD, and most important, bringing them to you in EYE-POPPING 3-D. It's like THE PAGES ARE TURNING RIGHT AT YOU!!! Because if there's one thing I know, it's everything. And if there are two things I know, it's that when 3-D movies make hundreds of millions of bucks their opening weekend, you copy that, no matter what the technological hurdles are. For instance, Hurdle Number One: 3-D movies are usually movies, not books. But did you know that *sometimes movies start out as books?* So until next summer's blockbuster movie *America Again: The Movie: Again Harder* comes out, put on the 3-D glasses in this envelope and cross over into a new dimension of sight and sound, especially if you read out loud.

In your face,

P.S. If you lose your 3-D glasses and would like a replacement pair, just bring $28.99 to your local bookstore, and they'll give you a new pair of glasses and a complimentary second copy of the book!

To everyone who bought this book

AMERICA

WRITTEN AND EDITED BY STEPHEN COLBERT RICHARD DAHM PAUL DINELLO BARRY JULIEN TOM PURCELL

AGAIN

WRITERS MICHAEL BRUMM ERIC DRYSDALE ROB DUBBIN GLENN EICHLER DAN GUTERMAN PETER GWINN
JAY KATSIR FRANK LESSER OPUS MORESCHI MEREDITH SCARDINO SCOTT SHERMAN MAX WERNER

RE-BECOMING THE GREATNESS

PRODUCED BY MEREDITH BENNETT ★ PHOTOGRAPHY BY ANDREW MATHESON

WE NEVER WEREN'T

SPECIAL THANKS TO ANDRO BUNETA NATE CHARNY MEGAN GEARHEART PAUL HILDEBRAND
BRENDAN HURLEY MATT LAPPIN KRISTOPHER LONG BILL MARKO ERICA MYRICKES

DESIGN BY DOYLE PARTNERS

TABLE OF CONTENTS

Dear Reader,

Thank you for purchasing this book. Before continuing, please read and agree to the following contract, which dictates this book's terms of use, your responsibilities in regard to copyright management, and dinner table etiquette. When you have agreed to the terms, you may continue installing the book into your mind (heretofore referred to as "reading").

Mark T. Adams
Burnham, Whitehead, Bronstein & Associates

TERMS AND CONDITIONS

The legal agreement set out below governs your use of *America Again: Re-becoming the Greatness We Never Weren't*. Please review them with your lawyer, loved ones, or beloved lawyer. If you do not agree to these terms, please return this book to your place of purchase. You will not receive a refund, but hopefully someone else will pick it up and enjoy it more than you.

A) COPYRIGHT MANAGEMENT

This book, and all images, text, and secret messages to hovering motherships, should be considered copyrighted material. Your appreciation of material contained within should be for personal use only. The reader cannot, will not, and most important, cannot copy any or all parts of this book, excluding the following made-up word: antedelopean.

Mere ownership of this book constitutes a non-disclosure agreement not to share the contents of the book with anyone. Describing this book to a group of more than 3 people, or less than 2, shall be considered a criminal act of piracy under the Digital Millennium Copyright Act. Describing it in an entertaining fashion shall be considered an unauthorized rebroadcast.

No parts of this book shall be "sampled" or "remixed" or "mashed-up" or "recontextualized" or "used as inspiration for" or "photocopied" or "borrowed from" or "used as source material" or "be nearby when working on a new project" or "homaged," or "thought about during sex as a way to delay orgasm."

This book may linger with the reader for 6 to 24 months after reading and affect one's actions. Therefore, purchasing this book gives Stephen Colbert exclusive rights to all books, movies, plays, paintings, photographs, light operettas, wood carvings, multimedia displays, new recipes for gumbo, dance maneuvers, pop songs, or orchestral works created while under the influence of the book. If works are created, Stephen Colbert should get top billing, or a co-creator credit, whichever is deemed more impressive.

The reader retains no rights to transfer this material to other devices, such as iPad, iPhone, PadPhone, Kindle, Kindle Fire, Kindle Sprindle, Paperback, Mass Market Paperback, Player Piano Scroll, Audiobook, Videobook, Odorbook, Snarky Post on Boing Boing, Braille, Zoetrope, Fortune Cookie Strip, or any other form of media in perpetuity throughout this or any other Universe.

Transgressions punishable by fine, jail time, or both.

B) TERMS OF SALE

This book (hereafter referred to as "this book") is to be purchased only at full price. If the buyer cannot afford the book at full price, the buyer is to get a job. I hear they're hiring down at the grocery store. I mean, sure, it's just as a bag boy, but you have to start somewhere. Look, when I was your age, I was a bag boy for two summers. It taught me a lot about dedication, hard work, and how much I hated being a bag boy. Those are lessons you can't buy. Well, *you* can't buy anything, because, apparently, you have no job.

All sales of products are as final as the cold, damp grave.

If this book has been taken out of a library, the borrower is immediately to call the library and pretend to have lost it, and offer to pay for the copy.

Transgressions punishable by flogging, caning, or both.

C) END-USER TERMS AND CONDITIONS

This book is intended for readers above the age of 18, or below the age of 18, or to be enjoyed on the reader's 18th birthday.

Readers of this book should be Americans in good standing, with little or no criminal record, who have pledged allegiance to their flag within the past 24 hours. Readers from any Axis of Evil countries (Iran, North Korea, Sweden) should stop reading immediately.

This book should not be read by illegal immigrants, or read aloud to one's children by illegal immigrants. If there is an emergency situation in which an illegal immigrant is the only person available to read aloud to one's children, care should be taken to pronounce the "J"s. Film composer "John Williams" should never sound the same as FoxNews pundit "Juan Williams."

Transgressions punishable by Hall, Oates, or both.

D) PHYSICAL TREATMENT OF BOOK

When reading in public, the book should be held at a 90-degree angle to the floor. If reading on a sloped surface such as a mountain or canyon wall, a variation of angle of one (1) degree is acceptable, if verified by a compass, plumb line, or certified autistic savant. Care should be taken not to cover up the photo, title, author, or publisher information on the front, rear, or spine of the book.

This book shall not be used as a trivet, hot plate, or coaster. The use of this book as a pillow is allowed, as long as the reader slips the book into a pillowcase of at least 400-thread count, and nothing sateen, because that's tacky.

Utensils are to be used in the American style *only*. When cutting meat, the fork is to be held in the left hand, tines down. After cutting your meat, set the knife down on the upper right quadrant of the plate, and transfer the fork to your right hand before eating.

E) PRIVACY POLICY

By reading this book, the reader agrees to allow Stephen Colbert access to and the right to boilerplate boilerplate boilerplate boilerplate lorem ipsum dolor amet Roy G Biv Bel Biv Devoe ABC BBD... are you seriously still reading this? You're supposed to look at all this tiny type and think, "Egad, I don't want whoever wrote that suing me!" But try being the guy who has to write it. It's a lot of words. Thousands of them. And you have to think about each one. It's tiring, man. And the whole time you're sitting there thinking, *No one's ever going to read this; it's just there to make people's eyes glaze over while surreptitiously stripping them of their rights.* And yet, here you are, reading. Fantastic. Thanks a lot, buddy. I guess that means I have to keep writing.

Well, fuck it. If I'm going to spend Sunday afternoon at the office while my family is celebrating my birthday at the water park, then I'll write what I want to write. Because neither my bosses nor the ass-captains at the publishing house are ever going to take the time to notice. Just you. Lucky, lucky you.

F) DREAMS

Yeah, I used to have them. And I can assure you they didn't involve generating Byzantine small-type legalese to protect some cocky TV host. I was going to travel. I was going to learn to play guitar. At the very least I was going to use my considerable writing skills—Walmont High Essay Contest Champion two years running, bitch!—to write something people would actually seek out, instead of rifle past impatiently with a vague sense of antediluvian tedium. (See what I meant about writing skills?) I was going to write the Great American Novel, or at least the Good American Novel. Amazon Top 1000. I'm not greedy. Give me a modest advance and a stern-but-lovable editor who's always *haranguing me for that copy!* and I will be happy. Is that too much to ask?

G) AND BY THE WAY

While we're talking about forgotten dreams, what about yours? We're six categories and 1300 words into this legal Sarlacc Pit, and you're not going anywhere. I'm getting the feeling you don't have a lot going on, either. Let me ask you something: have you ever seen a girl naked? I mean in person, and not for pay. Don't answer, I don't really want to know. I'm depressed enough right now. Let me just say this: there's a big world out there, buddy, full of interesting and exciting people—and yes, charitable women who will show you the goods with surprisingly little prompting. Why not put down the magnifying glass and give it a shot? You'll be surprised what a little sunlight can do for that acne.

H) THE SECOND-TO-LAST ONE

Let's put the both of us out of our misery, shall we? Because I've reached my word count and that means that, however mind-numbing and utterly inconsequential my day's work has once again been, at least now I get to go home and finish that bottle of Bushmills.

I) PRESUMPTION OF AGREEMENT

By either reading this section, or skipping it due to its minuscule font size, the reader agrees to the entirety of the contract, regardless of whether or not they choose to agree or not below. The reader cannot escape from the gravitational pull of this black-hole contract. There is no exit. This contract is a windowless, doorless room. You belong to the contract now.

Transgressions punishable by Strunk, White, or both.

❑ I have read and agree to this book's terms and conditions.

YES   OK

AMERICAN EXCEPTIONALISM

fig 19.3-D. **STEPHEN COLBERT**

CHAPTER ONE

AMERICAN EXCEPTIONALISM

"USA! USA! USA!"
—*America*

I wrote another book.[1] I hope you're happy. Because this book is your fault.[2] You see, everywhere I go I hear bellyaching about how we as a nation have lost it. Now sure, we've taken some shots lately. We're feeling beat up, and why wouldn't we? It's like after 235 years as King of the Monkey Bars, the other kids have held us down and made us eat a bug.

But the Real Question is: are America's best days behind us? Of course they are, and always have been. We have the greatest history in the history of History. But never forget, our best days are also ahead of us, and always will be. Because America also has the Greatest Future in the history of the Future. It's our Present that's the problem…and always is be.

Well, that ends now. This book is going to put America back on track, where it always will have been.

"But," you're thinking, "all the facts say that America is in decline." First of all, who told you to *think?*

Since Day One of *The Report*, I've said, "I don't want you to think, I want you to *feel*." Because if you think about America, sure we're neck-deep in debt, we're knee-deep in neck, and the dollar isn't worth the dime it's printed on.

---

[1] By the way, I'm really liking footnotes this time. Could just be a phase. No promises.

[2] The "you" I mean is any straight, non-atheist American. If you are not a citizen or are reading this book translated into another language and/or gay code, drop it and wait patiently for the proper authorities to arrive and pepper spray you.

FIGURE ONE: USA! USA! USA!

That's why I'm asking you to *feel* about America. Really *feel*. So please, close your eyes when you're reading this book. Are they closed? Good, let's continue.

America is Exceptional.

Does that statement shock you? It shocks me to even have to say it. To be forced by your doubt to say out loud that America is exceptional implies something ugly. It's like telling the host of a dinner party, "I'm certain your wife is a female." Saying it out loud feels wrong, no matter how large her hands are. Plus, the word "is" shouldn't even be in there. It's putting too much distance between "America" and "Exceptional."

Americeptional.

That's better. Plus it saves time. Time we could be spending with *our kids*.

I hear what you're feeling. "But Steven, is America really exceptional? The world is full of countries. I'm sure a lot of them are pretty good." First of all, it's "Ste*ph*en." Second, yeah, if countries are your "thing," I'm sure there are thousands of countries out there. You want to live in a country, move some place else. You want to live in America, this is the only game in town. As Newt Gingrich once pinched out:

COUNTRIES THAT ARE AMERICA
GUAM 0.5%
AMERICA
100%
MARGIN OF ERROR: +/- 1 GUAM

{ *"America's greatness, America's <u>exceptional</u> greatness, is not based on that fact that we are the most powerful, most prosperous—and most generous—nation on earth. Rather, those things are the <u>result</u> of American Exceptionalism."*[3]

---

[3] *A Nation Like No Other*, 2011, Newt Gingrich, front cover flap. Colbert Penny Saver: Read the first eight pages for free on Amazon. You'll get the gist.

Amen! America is Exceptional because of our Greatness and the source of all that Greatness is how Exceptional we are.

THE AMERICAN DREAM

And the entire world knows we're exceptional—and not just because we give them a steady supply of losing Super Bowl™ team t-shirts and sit-coms about doughy guys with hot wives.

We are an unwavering beacon of limitless freedom,[5] which people the world over see and say, "I want to live there. I want to be an American." That's why we must erect a 40-foot-high, 2,000-mile-long, 10,000-volt electric fence to keep those people out. There's only so much limitless freedom to go around!

Ronald Reagan said it first:[6] "America is the shining city upon a hill." And no matter how dark our days, or how low we sink, we will always be shiny and hilly. Reagan also said, "I have always believed that there was some divine plan that placed this great continent between two oceans to be sought out by those who were possessed of an abiding love of freedom and a special kind of courage." He's right, America was put here by God for us to find.[7]

HE SAID A LOT OF THINGS

AMERICAN EXCEPTIONALISM:
AN EXCEPTIONAL AMERICAN HISTORY

So just who came up with the term "American Exceptionalism"? Well, as you might guess, such a wholesome, all-American concept was invented by a regular Joe...seph Stalin. You see, back in 1927, American Communists complained to their leader that Communism could never work here because we had too many resources for the proletariat to rise up. Stalin mocked the idea by calling it "American Exceptionalism." All I'm saying is, Stalin had some good ideas. We proved ourselves to be exceptional, and defeated Communism. Now all that is left of Stalin is the phrase "American Exceptionalism" and, of course, his roaming, sentient mustache, which still visits bad little boys and girls who don't say "under God" in the Pledge of Allegiance.

I AM COMING FOR YOU.

---

[4] USA! USA!

[5] I'm still into that footnote thing. Could be here to stay.

[6] Paraphrasing JFK, who was paraphrasing John Winthrop, who was paraphrasing Jesus. Point is, I believe Reagan will return someday.

[7] Much like dinosaur bones.

America was like the sculpture existing inside the block of marble, waiting for the Artist to chip away a few Cherokee to find it.

Some people don't believe in American Exceptionalism.[8] Some people won't stand up for America.[9] They think that there are things in our history to be ashamed of. But I'm sorry, America is good at everything, except one thing: apologizing. Why should we apologize? Everything we've ever done has ended up creating the greatest country in the world, ergo[10] everything we did was the best possible choice. Besides "hindsight is 20/20." What does that mean? I don't know. We'll have to wait until the year 2020 to find out.[11]

ONE COLLEGE CREDIT

But ask yourself, what would America have been like if it had been run by the lefty apologists from the get-go? Would we have grown into an agricultural powerhouse without our Unpaid African Internship Program? No! Would we have conquered the West if we had over-regulated the Pioneers? No! And who wants their Good Crowned by Brotherhood "from Sea to shining Scranton?"

Throughout human history, countries rise and fall. But not America—we continue to rise and rise, like dough, until Jesus bakes us in the fiery Afterscape of the Rapture.[12] I don't know about you,[13] but I feel like if there were a better place, **GOD WOULD HAVE PUT ME IN IT.**[14]

The point is, America has faced hardships in the past, but we have always mounted a comeback worthy of a major motion picture starring Matt Damon. We defeated the Nazis. We defeated the Native Americans. We defeated the environment. We even defeated the Metric System. Kilos? Sorry, that's drug talk. This is America, where we eat Fruit by the Foot, not Muesli by the Meter!

---

[8] Looking at you, Microsoft Word spell check! Time to recognize "Exceptionalism!"

[9] These people are called Ameriplegics.

[10] It's Latin for "I'm right."

[11] Your move, Mayans!

[12] Best part, America comes pre-buttered!

[13] Just a turn of phrase. I know a lot about you.

[14] I'm thinking footnotes are over. I'm more into putting things in **bold** now. **DEAL WITH IT.**

So we're not going to think or apologize our way out of our current funk—we've got to genuinely *feel* that America is the greatest, freest, bestest nation God ever gave man on the face of this Earth. And we've got to let Her know we feel it.

You see, America is a Lovely Lady.[15] Right now, too many people are looking at America and saying, "Wow, honey, you've really let yourself go." They want Her to put on the "fat pants" of Socialism.

And hey, I'm not blind. I know America's got a little junk in the trunk. She's no longer a trim 13 colonies. But that's just more of Her to love. She'll only be as pretty as you make Her feel. Boost Her confidence. Tell

Her She's beautiful from Her Purple Mountains to Her Amber Waves.[16]

And, let's be honest, do you think you're such a catch? Would it kill you to dress up for Her? Put on a tie. Or at the very least, make sure your sweatpants match your Crocs.[17]

By reading this book you are renewing your vows with This Great Nation. Give Her the time and attention She needs, and fellas, you will get lucky.[18]

And we all will be *America Again!* [19]

---

[15] Footnotes are back!

[16] Is she a natural amber? Yes! The curtains match the grain.

[17] That's nothing compared to what Brazil would ask you to do.

[18] But don't ask Her to do that *thing*. She's not into it.

[19] *Re-Becoming the Greatness We Never Weren't* by Stephen Colbert!

JOBS

fig 20.3-D. **STEPHEN COLBERT**

CHAPTER TWO

JOBS

"I'M TAKIN' WHAT THEY'RE GIVIN',
'CAUSE I'M WORKIN' FOR A LIVIN'!"
—*Huey Lewis and the*
Pulitzer Prize–winning News

America is home to the greatest, most productive, best jobs in the history of mankind. And that's not just patriotic hyperbole. It's the finest, greatest, number one patriotic hyperbole ever! American jobs built this country, which explains why it took 236 years and cost us a fortune.[1] American jobs built the Interstate Highway System, Transcontinental Railroad, and the Erie Canal—*the greatest canal in the world.* Sorry, Ear Canal.

And American jobs are still the corner-stone of this great nation. They harvest our crops. They manufacture our cars. They Jamba our Juice. And they come in all types. There are jobs that work your brain. Jobs that work your hand. Jobs that work your rim. And American jobs teach us to appreciate time with our families, by leaving us so little of it. But our kids understand that jobs must come first. Right, I want to say...*Brian?* [2]

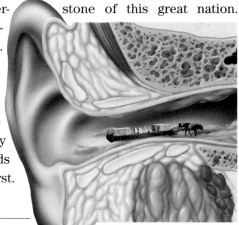

EARWAX: A HAZARD TO
NAVIGATION

---

[1] Seriously, couldn't we have just hired some Mexicans?
[2] For the record, my son's name is not Brian. I didn't forget it.
    I am pretending to forget it to protect the privacy of, I want to say...*Brendan?*

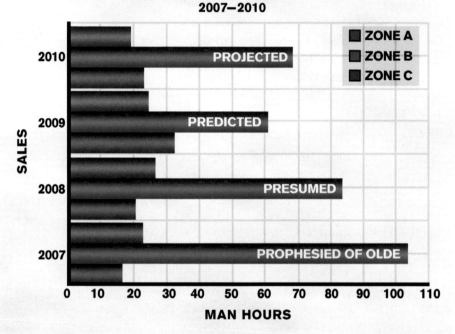

**UNIT SALES TARGET RATIOS
PER MAN-HOUR ANNUM
(EXCLUDING VARIABLE QUOTIENT)
2007–2010**

IMPORTANT-LOOKING GRAPH TO MAKE IT SEEM LIKE YOU'RE WORKING

And if you don't believe that our jobs are the greatest, then how do you explain the fact that you've been reading this book in your cubicle for the last hour, and haven't been fired? And make no mistake, a lot of people have been fired. Right now more than 13 million Americans are out of work. To put that into perspective: If you were to lay every unemployed American end to end, they would let you, if you paid them.

Those numbers translate to a jobless rate of anywhere from 5 to 40%, depending on math. (See graph). That is anywhere from unacceptable to unthinkable, with unbelievable and untenable jammed

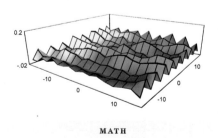

MATH

in between. Our customer service jobs are being outsourced to India. Our manufacturing jobs are being outsourced to China. And our complaining-about-losing-work-to-India-and-China jobs are being outsourced to Guatemala.[3] This level of joblessness is unprecedented, with the exception of Reconstruction,

JIMMY CARTER

WORK IT, GIRL!

the Great Depression, the mid-'70s, and the early '80s. Those last two don't have cool capitalized names, so we'll call them The Disco Downturn and Jimmy Carter's Poisoned Peanut.

True, the unemployment rate has been higher. In 1933, it peaked at 25%, with the other 75% working as "Heartbreaking Okie" models.

But back then unemployment was a career. It took training and dedication to ride the rails, cook beans, and die of tetanus. Plus, FDR was handing out those cushy make-work projects like painting Post Office murals, digging the Grand Canyon, and World War II-ing. That last one sent a bunch of our workforce overseas, and we had to try some bold new ideas, like letting women take jobs. (See: Rosie the Riveter.)

HISTORY'S MOST THINLY-VEILED LESBIAN—I HAVE WORKED HARD TO REMAIN IGNORANT OF WHATEVER DEPRAVED ACT "RIVETING" IS.

Meanwhile, we're four years into this current economic slump, and our nation's pop stars have yet to release a single Hobo song. During the 1930s, you couldn't step out your door without hearing a squeezebox rendition of "Big Rock Candy Mountain."

WHERE ARE THE HOBO SONGS, BEYONCE?!

SUGGESTED TITLES

ALL OUTTA BEANS

BINDLE STIXX

R U GONNA (FINISH THAT ROLL?)
as Sasha Fierce

---

[3] They are a tiny, bitchy people.

Today, Americans just aren't making the most of their despair the way our parents and grandparents did. Life is giving us lemons, and we're shipping them to China to make lemon-flavored lead-o-nade. And those Chinese will do it. Because everyone in the world wants an American job.

Now, let me make one thing perfectly clear. When I say American jobs, I don't mean American workers. American workers are a dime a dozen. Or they were until they unionized. These days, the American worker only performs the job for his own selfish needs like food, shelter, and accessible fire exits. Time was, American workers showed up at Ellis Island

"ATSA SPICYA LAND OFA OPPORTUNITY!"

with a dream in their heart, a shovel in their hand, and a potato in their pocket. They never asked for anything in return. And do you know why? Because they couldn't speak English!

The American job isn't thinking about itself; the American job only wants to get the job done. American workers have let our jobs down! It's no surprise our jobs left after the way we treated them! If I were jobs, I'd go where the workers know how to please jobs. Just look at the Tech Support page of the Kama Sutra. In India, there's no such thing as overtime. Just tantric clerking.

"HI! THIS IS MARY. PLEASE INSERT YOUR THUMB DRIVE."

THE PROTESTANT WORK ETHIC

Now, I may be a Catholic,[4] but I admire the Protestant work ethic. It'll really come in handy when they're shoveling coal in Hell, which is how the angels keep heaven heated to exactly 72 degrees for us Catholics. The problem with America today is that we have forgotten what the Puritan forefathers knew.

The Puritans believed that hard work, frugality, and worldly success were signs you were already one of God's elect— a person predestined to go to heaven. This gave them a single-minded focus on achieving the Reward they had already achieved.

They were a people that made things, and then put buckles on those things. They even put buckles on their hats. That's right, **they worked so hard, they needed to buckle down their hats.** The only thing the Puritans didn't make was love, because the late night hours were prime bucklin' time.

MODEL PROTESTANT

PROFILES IN FASTENING

THE VIRTUOUS BUCKLE

THE DEVIL'S CLOSURES

THE BOASTFUL BUTTON
A sign of vanity and pride. Show some humility and cover those threadholes!

THE SLUTTY SNAP
A male AND female side? Why not just **hump** your shirt closed?!

VELCRO: NASA DOES THE NASTY
Sure. Just slap two strips together any which way. No names!

ZIPPER: JAWS OF SATAN
Anyone who's gotten their tender bits caught in one of these knows that easy access has its price.

---

[4] No "maybe" about it. I'm the Buddha of Catholics.

These grim joyless automatons got up at dawn, buckled their hats, and headed out for a long day of deforesting the continent, removing stones to stack into picturesque fences, and removing Indians to stack into picturesque piles of dead Indians. And they were rewarded by God with land and wealth—at least until their neighbors accused them of witchcraft or they were hanged for being insufficiently buckled on a Sunday.

And this work ethic carried us through the Industrial Revolution, when we finally made things that made other things. Tragically, we had to stop wearing buckles, because they tended to get caught in the spindle reaper.

ALL TIME FAVORITE LUTHERS

Need an example of the Protestant work ethic? Just look at their religion's founder, **MARTIN LUTHER**. I'm no fan, but let's give the Devil his due. He posted 95 Theses to the door of the Catholic Church. Most people these days would stop at, like, 12 theses, tops. And this was back before the Internet, so he couldn't even look up "plenary indulgences" on Wikipedia. Which is why I put him ahead of Luther Vandross on my list of Favorite Luthers.

5. LEX LUTHOR

4. LUTHER VANDROSS

3. MARTIN LUTHER

2. MARTIN LUTHER KING JR

1. LEX LUTHOR KING JR.[5]

JOB CREATORS

COLB QUIZ | **WHAT IS AMERICA'S GREATEST RESOURCE?** | Ⓐ Get back to work. Ⓑ The answer is "Job Creators." Ⓒ Tungsten!
FOR ANSWER, SEE BELOW.

If you expect me to give you the answer, you've proven my point: America is in decline thanks to shiftless quiz-respondents looking for answer-handouts. If instead of waiting for a hint, you read the quiz, put down the book, went out and founded a steel company, guided it to success using nothing but your own motive power, made hyper-aggressive love to a gorgeous railroad magnate whom you regard with cold respect verging on hatred, then PAID a worker of inferior intellect to answer the quiz, then you, like me, are a Job Creator. I'm honored that you're reading this book. Though, if you were truly self-reliant, you would have written it yourself.

[5] He has been to the mountaintop...*that he created with an earthquake machine! You fools!*

I'll explain. There are two types of people on this planet. I'll explain more. Type One is the Job Creators: self-sufficient, self-motivated egotists, who produce works of industry, art, philosophy, and punditry, not for others' enjoyment but *as an end in themselves.* Yes, that was so important I underlined the period. When Henry Ford invented the old-timey car, when Aristotle invented thinking, when Alexander Graham Bell invented the Teddy Graham, they were not prompted by a social-istic desire to "serve their fellow man." They were pursuing a self-generated drive to make manifest an unborrowed vision of total independence, or in Aristotle's case, to tag anything in a short toga.

WHAT ARE YOU GONNA DO? HE HAD TENURE.

If that doesn't describe you, I am not sorry to inform you that you are the second type of person: a Parasite. For more, I quote The Great Ayn Rand:

"Any man using the words of another is an unthinking Parasite worthy of contempt and death." —AYN RAND

Smart lady. And if what I'm told is true, she rocked Alan Greenspan's balls.

But there's no shame in being a Parasite, because only a Job Creator can experience an emotion as complex as shame. Parasites, on the other hand, feel vague and inchoate *needs*:

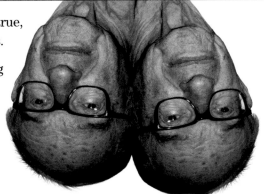

VISUAL APPROXIMATION OF
ALAN GREENSPAN'S SCROTUM

the *need* for paved roads, the *need* for clean drinking water, the *need* for your burning home to be put out.

But most despicable of all may be the Parasite's *need* to give to charity. Have you ever wondered why folks enjoy handing their personal earnings to the poor? It never made sense to me, until I sat down and figured it out the way a Job Creator does, using reason-thoughts. Turns out, Parasites give to charity in order to feel superior to those with less. "Ha ha," they think as they hatefully

ME, ME, ME, ME, ME!

scribble their checks, "You need a malaria net, and I do not!" There is nothing greedier than an act of so-called altruism. You share your food with your children not out of a make-believe sense of selflessness, but to remind them that you're the Big Food Man. Well, I respect my children enough to demand that in return for food that *I* paid for, they make the mutually beneficial exchange of tuck-pointing my chimney. Those Pop Tarts are all the sweeter for the knowledge that they *earned* them with their own grout-gnarled hands.

You've probably heard the fable of the Ant and the Grasshopper, but you can't trust Aesop's version because he was a slave, therefore mooching off the teat of his Forced-Job-Creator. So here's how it should have gone down:

THE AYNT AND THE GRASSHOPPER

ONCE UPON A TIME there was an ant—a virile ant. An ant who took what he wanted and did not apologize for his success. There was also a pitiable and insecure grasshopper, who incidentally was not a very good architect. During summer, the grasshopper fiddled all day. Meanwhile, the ant wrote a beautiful symphony for strings and then burned the sheet music so he would be the only one to ever enjoy its beauty.

When winter came, the ant was holed up in his warm cottage, with plenty of food, while the foolish grasshopper was slowly starving to death in the cold. The ant heard a knock on his door, but it wasn't the grasshopper, it was a cricket, the ant's conscience. "Look into your heart and take pity on the grasshopper, for he is starving," the cricket pleaded.

The ant and the cricket were then crushed by the foot of Ayn Rand, because the way the ants all worked together in their colony reminded her of Socialism.

THE BEGINNING!

But Americans today don't appreciate that you have to work for what you get. And as the world has gotten smaller, our ability to thrive in the global marketplace has been compromised by one thing:

UNIONS

Unions' impossible rule makes it too expensive to manufacture anything in America. Case in point: this book. It was hand-sewn by Bangladeshi toddlers. American workers just don't have hands small enough to manually typeset the tiny footnotes.[6]

From the get-go, workers rights were a regulatory overreach by weaklings who couldn't handle putting in an honest 185-hour workweek. Yes, there are only 168 hours in a week, so their employers would generously loan them the extra 17 hours, and their children would repay it by disentangling the threshing teeth of the wool mangle.

GOMPERS, SEEN HERE
FAILING TO EAT A MARMOT

HE WAS NEVER TOLD

But that was all ruined when in 1866, after a series of shoemaker, railroad, carpenter, miner, and mill worker protests, the American Federation of Labor was formed, headed by Samuel Gompers. Worst of all, these strikes provoked violence, like the Great Railroad Strike of 1877 where workers were attacked by the Maryland militia; the Chicago Haymarket riot of 1886 where anarchists lobbed dynamite at police; and the Writers' Guild of America Strike of 2007, where the writing staff of *According to Jim* was hacked to death by machete-wielding TV critics.

Worst of all, Onions[9] led to:

---

[6] Thanks for nothing, American child labor laws! [7]

[7] And thanks for typesetting that footnote, Korean tweens! [8]

[8] This footnote was typeset by a Laotian preemie.

[9] Sorry, that should read "Unions." English is the second language of my non-union Malaysian editor.

REGULATIONS

From the moment we wake up not on fire to the moment we fall back asleep with all our fingers, Americans are hampered by needless regulations. We've become a Nanny State, and not the good type of nanny that lets you watch Cinemax, eat ice cream out of the carton, and take cigarettes from her purse.[10]

Americans are drowning in a sea of regulations—or at least we would be drowning, if Big Government didn't force us to wear life jackets.

Now, when I sold you this book, I trusted you could handle the responsibility of a hardcover. But that's not what Joe Government thinks. (Note: Joe Government is a character I have invented that will soon be the villain of his own psychosexual suspense trilogy. Think *Girl with the Dragon Tattoo*, except no girls or tattoos. Still trying to work in the dragons.) He's worried you'll cut yourself on the pages, or drop the heavy hardcover on your toe, or lick the poison flavor-strip on the cover.[11]

Remember: our Founding Fathers didn't have onerous regulations weighing them down. They did what they pleased, when they pleased, with whom they pleased, until they died from eating tainted meat at age 32. Pursuit of Happiness!

Point is, regulation is a jobs killer—emission standards, waste management requirements, that one law that prohibits howler monkeys from running an H-R department.

BOBO NEEDS YOU TO FILL OUT YOUR START PAPERWORK AGAIN. HE ATE IT.

---

[10] I'll never forget you, Mrs. Freudenthal.

[11] If they've taken the poison flavor-strip off the cover, the battle has already been lost.

This regulatory tsunami is creating a climate of fear that is keeping American business leaders from hiring. Who knows what job-killing regulation will be passed next? A new Nocturnal Emissions Standard? Extended Fraternity Leave?

Everything started going downhill the day we introduced our nation's first minimum wage back in 1938. Guaranteeing hourly pay not only hurts worker productivity, but worker self-esteem! How is an employee supposed to gauge his true value to the company if he knows his employer is *forced* to pay him $7.25 an hour? And calling that a "minimum" wage is a misnomer. I bet I can think of a lot of wages lower than that—$6.11… $5.24… $2.43…and others.

And when regulations aren't strangling jobs, they're useless. Let me give you an example. Just last night, I was in a restaurant,[12] and there was a sign in the restroom that said "Employees Must Wash Hands." I waited for nearly a half-hour. No employee showed up to wash my hands. Even when I tracked one down and insisted, they did it begrudgingly, and let's just say, it was a less-than-thorough job.

So to combat the jobs we have lost to China, I am proposing what I call "Colbert Opportunity Zones"—regulation-free areas to be set up across the country.

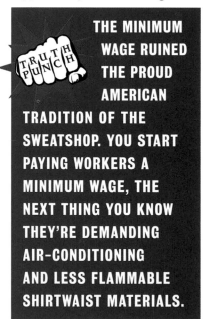

THE MINIMUM WAGE RUINED THE PROUD AMERICAN TRADITION OF THE SWEATSHOP. YOU START PAYING WORKERS A MINIMUM WAGE, THE NEXT THING YOU KNOW THEY'RE DEMANDING AIR-CONDITIONING AND LESS FLAMMABLE SHIRTWAIST MATERIALS.

Businesses would be free to employ whomever they want, to do whatever they need. If you can fit in a mineshaft, you have a job. If you make it back out, you have a career. This lack of regulation will lead to countless steady, good-paying jobs, a booming economy, and Thunderdomes where drifters fight to the death with broken umbrella handles.[13]

Imagine a country without unions. Where every American has the opportunity to compete with a 7-year-old for a job. Every morning, each American would go to work. Every night, many of them would return. But I promise you this: the on-job fatality rate would *never* outgrow the birth rate. And isn't that what's truly important? The children?

---

[12] No matter when you are reading this, last night I was in a restaurant.

[13] Any broken handle will do. Let's not over-regulate.

I FEEL YOUR PAIN

But don't fret, unemployed nation, because I, Stephen Colbert, feel your pain. I've been in your shoes. They got switched at a bowling alley.

When I left *The Daily Show* I thought I'd never work again. I felt like a loser. I slipped into a depressive spiral. I started doing drugs, gained 40 pounds, and pushed away a lot of good friends who were just trying to help. But three hours later, I landed a job at a new show: *The Colbert Report*.

Still, not a day goes by when I don't remember those three hours. Every night when I close my eyes, my job suddenly disappears. Also, the rest of the world—which is scary. And because I know what it's like to not know where your next paid vacation is coming from, I am here to help you get back on the job horse.

THEY WERE HORRIBLE. NO ARCH SUPPORT.

GETTING A JOB

Let's get you working! Let's see, currently in America there is… one job opening: Junior shampoo boy at Jackie's Hairtacular in Reno, Nevada. You're gonna get it! As long as you have the perfect résumé.

SIMPLE RULE TO REMEMBER: WHEN YOU RÉSUMÉ, YOU MAKE A RÉS OF U AND MÉ

Today, a job applicant needs a résumé like a fish needs a Jet Ski—it's essential if you're going to beat the other salmon upstream. This is the potential employer's first impression of you. Now, consulting a career coach to craft the perfect résumé can be expensive. Luckily, I'm here to help with my patented

STÉPHÉN T. CÓLBÉRT RÉSUMÉ ÁSSÍSTÁNTÉ!

A LOSING RÉSUMÉ

Always put an address in the nicest part of town, which will have a Super 8 instead of a Motel 6. You know it's better because the number is higher.

Don't just list your e-mail. Show that you're on the cutting edge of communication by listing your Twitter account, Google Voice number, Tumblr page, and possible future communication devices, such as Hologram Avatar, Gunglepussr Handle, and Neural Synapse Antenna Code.

Ned B. Jobless
126 Sycamore Way
Jobville, USA 12334
(555) 555-62332
Gary.resumeberg@xprqx.com

Remember, you can get the big call about a job day or night. So, from the minute you apply for a job, NEVER GO TO SLEEP. Caution: After three days, you may hallucinate that you've been hired.

OBJECTIVES: Honestly, you could stop there.

To find employment in a sales position with a company that allows me to utilize my skills, attention to detail, and leadership abilities to increase sales and profitability.

On second thought, this whole "need a job thing" makes you sound kind of desperate. Play it coy. Start sentences with "Not that I'm looking but..." Or under OBJECTIVES, just write, "Wouldn't you like to know?"

EXPERIENCE:

Worked? We know you worked. *It was work.* This sounds weak. Always make your job sound vital by using strong action verbs like Jack-hammered, Wind-Sprinted, Sucker-Punched, Heimliched, and NASCARed.

Senior Group Sales Representative

InsuraMed Health Insurance Corporation   2007–2010

Worked to increase sales to large-group clients and manage ongoing corporate accounts. Supervised team of three sales representatives. Trained new hires.

This applicant wasn't working between 2010-2012. Employers don't like unemployment gaps, so fill it by any means necessary. Give yourself a job title for that period such as Supervising Remote Control Specialist or Senior Vice Chair of Waving Length of Yarn at Cat.

BO-Ring! Where's the zazz? End the description with something that will grab their attention, like, "Managed expense reports, routinely nabbed chemical weapons cache from clutches of the Haqqani network."

Sales Representative, Investment Division

J.T. Hayland Financial Services   2004–2006

Maintained relationship with ongoing clients.

Increased revenues in each of 10 quarters.

Also, be sure to list any Unfair Hiring Practices lawsuits you've won. This will help establish you as a take-charge person, who will sue them if they don't hire you.

This is good! People like juice. Try to include the word "JAMBA" in other parts of this resumé. For instance, punch-up the previous item: "JAMBAed relationship with ongoing clients. Increased juice in each of 10 JAMBAs."

Sales Associate

Jamba Juice   2001–2004

Prepared and provided customers with juice and related products.

This section is too short. You only went to one school? That doesn't sound smart. Pump this up. List all of your schooling: summer school, Sunday school, home school, Schoolhouse Rock, rappers you've been personally schooled by, and any college sweatshirt you own. In fact, wear one to the interview!

EDUCATION:

Amherst College, 1999   Amherst, MA

B.A. in Sociology

Nothing says, "I majored in bong hits" like a Sociology degree. Change that to 'Law.' If they ask follow-up questions, take the Fifth. They'll be impressed by your expertise.

Don't just list software—list all electronics you know how to use, like toasters and clock radios. You don't just hit a snooze button, you operate highly sensitive sleep extension technology!

SKILLS:

Microsoft Office, Adobe Photoshop, Mac and Windows.

Fluent in Spanish.

Never admit to knowing another language. It says that you're willing to cheat on English.

HOBBIES AND INTERESTS:

Community Service: volunteer at local soup kitchen,

Big Brother program, and ASPCA.

Don't list hobbies, unless your hobby is "Continuing to work." Donating coats to kids in your spare time only reminds employers that you have spare time. Remember this simple rhyme, "If you have time to donate, you have time to stay late!"

REFERENCES:

Available upon request.

Pick the most famous people who have died in the past month as your references. They can't check on this!! I got my show thanks to the warm endorsement of Pope John Paul II.

This is also a good place to indicate how much you can bench press. I always have at least one person on staff who can lift my desk off me in case of an earthquake.

Do not doodle your favorite band names in the margin, unless you're applying to be a roadie—which is a waste of time anyway, since those jobs are chosen not by résumé, but by ponytail length.

Alex J. Attaboy[14]
201 Mansion Place
Jobtown, USA

SUMMARY: Let's cut the crap. Put the résumé down. Stop playing grab-ass and just call me for an interview.

OBJECTIVE: Not that I'm looking, but it seems like you guys could use someone awesome, because right now instead of counting money, you're reading résumés. What's *your* objective? Whatever happened to that dream of sailing around the world? You should quit. And then, I guess, my objective would be your job.

LEADERSHIP QUALITIES:

- Have bullhorn, am white male
- Often say "Walk with me"
- Thought to include "Leadership Qualities" section
- Studied Hitler's rise to power (will use for good not evil)
- Motivating co-workers with subliminal compliments — Speaking of which, have you lost weight? You look a-mazing!

EXPERIENCE:

Coma Patient 2010-2012
- Responsible for autonomic and healing processes of human body
- Definitely not out of work for 2 years, which is hard to justify on a résumé
- Triumphed over odds

Banksy 2005-2010
- Yes, the secret's out, I'm the world-renowned anonymous street artist.
- Responsible for blowing the doors off the art world
- Pushed boundaries while exploring themes of anarchy and capitalism
- Some light filing

Home Office Manager 1999-2005
- Responsible for overseeing maintenance of operations of one-bedroom apartment
- Composed freelance television reviews, delivered to friends via wireless telecom
- Additional duties included Halogen Lightbulb Installer, Burrito Microwave Technician, and Pornography Monitor

---

[14] JAMBA!

Senior Executive of Energy Extraction and Delivery,
Jamba Juice Worldwide   1997-1999
- Headed up one-man division of product preparation and disbursement
- Intense interaction with corporate and individual clients
- Managed thrice-daily lavation of commercial surfaces utilizing state-of-the-art O-Cedar implements
- Put up with Terry's shit for 8 months, which believe me, is an impressive feat. Ask Rick.

EDUCATION:

Harvard University, Yale Campus, 1999   Princeton, NJ
B.A. in Dartmouth Studies, graduated Summa Cum Stanford

CNBC on mute, Fitness World, 2011   Wayne, PA
Watched a ton of CNBC on overhead TV while on the elliptical. Can't say what the stories were about but noticed the ticker said something about the DOW rallying by closing.

Uncle Gary, Thanksgiving, 1987   Norristown, PA
Cornered me in garage and told me how the world "really" works. Learned that it's all about who you know. The whole damned system is corrupt from the inside out. Plus, Nixon got a bad rap. The Watergate scandal overshadowed the many great, perfectly legal things Nixon did to sabotage the Democrats.

Repeated exposure to Bach, 1976   Womb

SPECIAL SKILLS:
- Gimme a blowtorch, a bottle of Absinthe, and a hula hoop — and I'll show you.
- JAMBAing

REFERENCES
- 28 Twitter followers
- 2 LinkedIn connections
- Rick
- 2 out of 8 former lovers
- Abraham Lincoln (see attached)

Letter of Recommendation

I'm not going to sugarcoat this: the job market is brutal, especially for entry-level sugarcoaters. But even if you have other skills, you know what they say: it isn't what you know, it's who you know. Well, congratulations! You know me—in the form of this book. To help you get a leg up in today's competitive job market, I've written you a letter of recommendation to bring to your next job interview. With this letter, a confident smile, and a firm handshake, you WILL land that job ... unless the other applicants have a copy of this book, too. So try to get that interview before Christmas 2012.

From the desk of Stephen T. Colbert

To whom it may concern:

Please consider this letter my personal recommendation for the great American worker standing/kneeling/weeping before you.

This candidate has consistently proven to be bright, highly motivated, well-organized, very efficient, consistently pleasant, extremely competent, remarkably responsible, extraordinarily assured, astonishingly flexible, inconceivably punctual, mind-bendingly polite, surprisingly athletic, impossibly charming, delightfully intelligible, giddily hygienic, uniquely distilled, and magically delicious.

He/she possesses first-rate communication skills and is always willing to share his/her knowledge with colleagues, unless this position requires confidentiality, in which case feel comfortable telling this worker your trade secrets, as well as your darkest fantasies/ATM PIN.

I can assure you that this worker excelled in school, both academically and by lettering in several sports that you also played. You definitely have a lot to talk about.

And this worker attained all his/her skills and positive personality traits in the face of great adversity, having grown up with or without an alcoholic parent/guardian/pet.

Besides routinely putting in an 80-hour week in addition to caring for a family of 1 to 6 members, this candidate also finds time to volunteer, working tirelessly to combat homelessness, hunger, environmental destruction, election fraud, education inequality, sweatshops (except yours), and DVD piracy. He/she performs these selfless good works without pay, without recognition, and often without permission.

Hire this hardworking American today! This candidate is not a stickler for the rules when it comes to office romance, and already kind of likes you!

Sincerely,

Stephen Colbert

PRE-EMPLOYMENT DRUG TEST
PEE ON THIS PAGE.

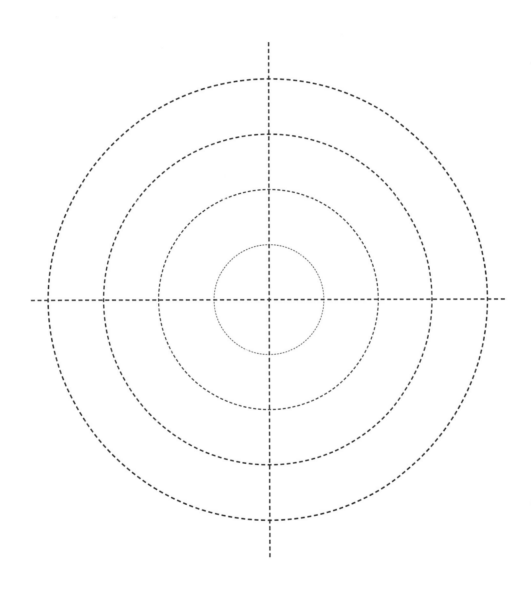

IF IT TURNS YELLOW, THEN YOU'RE HIGH.
WHY ELSE WOULD YOU PEE ON A BOOK?

How to
HANDLE YOUR JOB INTERVIEW

Congratulations! If you followed my résumé advice, you've already landed a job interview, especially if you also followed my advice to make sure your grandfather went to Brown with the company's boss. (If you didn't, it's not too late for Gramps to disguise himself as a 19-year-old and join the right

secret society. For pointers, see my unpublished screenplay "Frat Grandpa.")

As you prepare for the interview, keep in mind at all times: If you fuck this up, you will never get another interview. This is your entire future, right here. Nailing this equals food for your children. Failure means giving out two-dollar handjobs at the bus station. This is do-or-die, and the pressure is cripplingly intense.

Also, remember to have fun!

JOB INTERVIEW IS LIKE A FIRST DATE. For it to go well, you should look your best, act confident, and if they pick up dinner, put out. Wear something loose. Here is a handy checklist to follow for the big day:

BEFORE THE INTERVIEW

1

DO YOUR RESEARCH.
Look up some facts about the company you're interviewing with, such as:
★ Their name
★ Their address
★ What they do or make

If you find anything incriminating, hold onto it for when you're negotiating your "salary."

2

PRACTICE, PRACTICE, PRACITCE. (SORRY, TYPO).
Conduct "mock interviews" with a friend.
Have them really push you until you learn:
★ What makes you cry?
★ What makes you take a swing at a friend?
★ When do you think life really begins?
★ Why can't you listen to Billy Joel's "The Longest Time" without breaking down in tears?

Trust me, you'd much rather find your breaking point with a friend than in a big office building with security guards and elevators that play Easy Listening hits from the '80s.

3

PREPARE YOUR OWN QUESTIONS.
An interviewer will frequently ask if you have any questions for them. Think about this, and have some at the ready.

Here are some suggestions:
★ What kind of place is this?
★ Who the FUCK do you think you are?
★ How about that area sports team?
★ Wuzzzuuuuuuuppp?
★ Are you wearing a wire?
   You have to tell me if you are.
★ What is the highest you've ever been?
★ No, where do *you* see *yourself* in five years?

Asking questions about the interviewer's personal interests is a great way to make a connection.

For example, if you see a framed photo of their children on their desk, you could ask, "So, you like putting photos in frames?"

OLBERT HELPFUL HINT:
FRAME THIS PHOTO, BRING IT WITH YOU TO THE INTERVIEW, AND PLACE IT ON YOUR SIDE OF THE DESK. BAM! PLAYING FIELD: LEVELED!

APPEARANCE

IT IS VITAL THAT YOU MAKE A GOOD impression in your interview by having a professional appearance. Ideally, you will pack up 10 different outfits in various degrees of formality, then camp out in the parking lot early, watching people walk into the office to see what they're wearing, and pick out the clothes that match the best. If during your surveillance you identify a current worker with a build and facial type closely resembling yours, a simpler route to employment may be to kidnap them, study their mannerisms, and then "replace" them. If neither of those options pans out, here are some general guidelines.

MEN *"Don't get cute. Wear a suit."* ™

If that's the case, your best bet is to go with an off-the-rack two-piece suit, preferably a charcoal gray or charcoal grey. Remember, you're applying to be assistant night manager of an Arby's, not a whorehouse.

TIE: Most interviewers frown upon being asked to help tie an applicant's tie during an interview, so be sure to stop by early to ask for their help.

SHOES: Wear some.

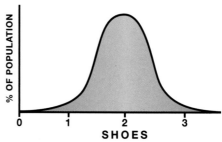

AVERAGE NUMBER OF SHOES NEEDED FOR JOB INTERVIEW

LADIES **BLOUSE:** Otherwise known as a "she-shirt." This should be silky and buttoned low enough to say "I'm a woman," but high enough to say, "I might be a lesbian."

PANTS: Your pants should be a skirt. You're not Katherine Hepburn! And if you are, what are you doing applying for a desk job? You should be back in the pictures! We miss you, Kate!

BRA: Make sure it fastens in the back, not the front. Those things are confusing, and you don't want to make the interviewer feel insecure.

APOLOGY: My editor is making me apologize for what I said about the bra. So: wear either, it's your choice.

HAIR: You have many options here, short hair or ONE ponytail at the BACK of your head.

GET IN THE EMPLOYER'S HEAD

When walking into an interview, remember that the employer wants you to succeed. If you're as good a fit as you seemed on your résumé, your interviewer can go home and/or start drinking early. So you already have a leg up the moment you walk in the door, except in the following circumstances:

❶ Your interviewer has been told they're going to be laid off as soon as they finish filling these job openings. **❷** There is no job and the interview is a complicated ruse to lure unsuspecting applicants into a confidence game. (See my unpublished screenplay "Nigerian Prince Grandpa.")

BEFORE THE INTERVIEW

★ Check in with the receptionist and remember to be courteous. He or she is the gatekeeper to the office, and very likely sleeping with the boss. There will be pillow talk, and you want your name to be panted favorably.

★ After you've given the receptionist your name and a knowing wink, find a seat in the waiting room. In all likelihood there will be several other applicants who have been sizing you up the whole time you were over there winking at the receptionist like an asshole. This is what is called "the snake pit," because it's all about playing head games and psyching out your enemy—*just like snakes do in a pit.*

★ Sow self-doubt in the minds of your rivals. For instance, you might casually say to your neighbor, "This job is my Make-A-Wish." Or "Can you believe they made us bring another stool sample? I have an extra, if you need one."

IAN MCKELLEN
IS
NIGERIAN PRINCE
GRANDPA

It's Time To Meet
The SCAM-Parents!

PRESCOTT PICTURES INC. IN ASSOCIATION WITH LOREM IPSUM A PRESCOTT PICTURES INC. PRODUCTION A STEPHEN COLBERT FILM IAN MCKELLEN WITH DOLORE MAGNA IN "NIGERIAN PRINCE GRANDPA" WRITTEN BY STEPHEN COLBERT DIRECTED BY STEPHEN COLBERT PRODUCED BY PRESCOTT PICTURES INC.
COMING SOON EXCLUSIVELY ON HD DVD

WHEN I'M INTERVIEWING A JOB CANDIDATE, HERE'S WHAT I'M LOOKING FOR:
Could I take them in a fistfight?
What if knives are involved?
Did they flinch? If so, two for flinching.

★ If mind games don't seem to work, pretend to bend down and tie your shoe, then use a letter opener to slice your neighbor's Achilles tendon. Then sprint to the bathroom and hide the weapon "prison style."

★ Another important consideration in waiting room strategy is your reading material. When your future employer enters, the first thing he or she will see is the magazine you've chosen. Be careful what message you send. *Us Weekly* or *People* says, "I reached my peak intellectual curiosity in second grade," while *The New Yorker* says, "I use words like *mise-en-scène* and *pied-à-terre*. Punch me."

GO TIME!

★ Once your future employer and future wrongful termination lawsuit defendant enters, you've got to be on your A-game. That means no texting and absolutely NO flossing your teeth, no matter how much that fajita steak fiber is totally killing you. Focus!

★ Maintain eye contact, but not to the point that it's creepy. Plan your blink rate ahead of time. About nine per minute is good. Don't count out loud, but moving your lips is OK.

★ Use honorifics like "Sir" or "Ma'am," but be sure you've determined your future employer's gender before settling on one. If this is not possible, use a gender-neutral honorific such as "Your Eminence" or "Thunder Thighs."

★ If your nerves get the best of you and you pass gas, blame it on the dog. Dogs are admittedly rare in interview situations. Those prone to bouts of nervous flatulence should plan ahead by pretending to be blind and bringing a seeing-eye dog. Also, make sure you and the dog share a common diet for a few weeks to ensure that the scent of your flatulence matches up.

WHAT DOES THE NUMBER OF SHAKES SAY ABOUT YOU?

ONE SHAKE
I'm a dainty princess whose porcelain hands can't handle the rigors of a full handshake—or a full-time job.

TWO SHAKES
I'm professional and courteous.

THREE SHAKES
I'm too professional and courteous. Probably hiding something.

FOUR SHAKES
I would like to "continue the interview" in my hotel room.

FIVE SHAKES
I am a water pump.

SIX+ SHAKES
I'm having a seizure. Call 911.

The HANDSHAKE

The importance of the handshake cannot be overstated. In fact, I could write—and have written—an entire book about it, albeit without a publisher.[15] To be sure you shake hands in as professional and awe-inspiring a manner as possible, follow these steps precisely:

1 FINGERS STRAIGHT, PALM DRY, SECOND THUMB SURGICALLY REMOVED.

2 EXTEND RIGHT HAND. (If you're left-handed, don't worry. There are plenty of jobs where your aberration is acceptable. Traveling freakshows typically hire in the winter months around Sarasota)

3 ELBOW AT 150 DEGREES—FEEL FREE TO BREAK OUT A PROTRACTOR.

4 CLASP HANDS, FEEL THE ELECTRICITY.

5 EYE CONTACT! FOCUS ON THE BLACK OF THE PUPIL. REMEMBER, YOU ARE HIGH-DIVING INTO HIS SOUL.

6 TWO FIRM SHAKES! (See sidebar)

7 QUICK RELEASE— NO FINGER-TRAILING OR PALM-TICKLING.

8 NOD WITH A SLIGHT GRIN, INDICATING THAT YOU EXPERIENCED THE SHARED MAGIC.

9 BLOW A KISS. A LITTLE ROMANCE NEVER HURT.

---

[15] *Easy as 1, 2, Squeeze! Learn To Shake in Five Weeks or Less!*

★ Almost as important as the handshake is remembering your future employer's name. I have since learned that it is helpful to use a mnemonic device to remember it. For instance, if the interviewer's name is Doug, remember **Dairy Octopus Under Glass**. Now try working those words into your interview answers: "**U**nder the right working conditions, I can shatter the **G**lass ceiling that has kept me down. I think your company will benefit from my experience in the **D**airy industry, where I invented a system to milk an **O**ctopus, Doug." Hired!

KEVIN

★ Alternately, make a point of repeating your interviewer's name as many times as possible as soon as you hear it. "Kevin, it's a pleasure to meet you, Kevin. Kevin could you tell me what the hours are like, Kevin? Tell me, Kevin! Kevin tell me! Kevin Kevin Kevin!!!"

The INTERVIEW

Once the interview starts, you're going to have a lot of questions thrown at you. Be prepared to answer honestly and thoughtfully, by memorizing these answers verbatim.

QUESTION:
"Tell me about yourself."
This is an intentionally open-ended, trick question designed to throw you off your game. The best way to handle this curveball is with the Keyser Söze method, using objects in the boss's office to improvise an answer. See a deer head on the wall? You love hunting. See a diploma from Vassar? Your middle name is Vassar. Is there a picture of his kids playing soccer? You're on their soccer team, too.

QUESTION:
"Where do you see yourself in five years?"
You don't want to just give the employer an answer here. You want to take him on a journey. "Where do I see myself in five years? Right here, sir. And the whole building is crumbling around us during a 9.6 earthquake. Everybody is screaming and panicking, but not me, sir. Not me. I'm hoisting you up and slinging you over my shoulder, fireman-style. I'm carrying you down the stairs, out to the street to safety. Then you'll turn to me and thank me. I'll say, 'For what, sir?' And you'll look me in the eye as a tear falls from yours and say, 'For keeping the promise you made to me five years ago when I hired you.'"

QUESTION:
"What attracts you to this line of work?"
The honest answer is, "It is a line of work." But that won't make you stand out. Here is where you need to show passion for the job. You LOVE whatever the company does. Sheet metal stamping? You've been doing it recreationally for years. Marine biologist? You were banned from Sea World for leaping into Shamu's tank. Accountant? Through your obsession with numbers you have discovered numerological patterns in the Bible that can predict the exact date and time when the warriors of Jesus will arrive on clouds of glory to judge the living and the dead—and there shall be weeping and gnashing of teeth.

QUESTION:
"Why did you leave your last job?"

You were not fired, you were not laid off. That immediately evokes an image of you trashing the break room. Always present this answer in such a way that you were in control of your destiny.

Examples:

"I wanted to explore other opportunities."

"I wanted to work for a REAL company."

"Got that ramblin' itch, know what I mean?"

If you're trying to get a job at a frozen yogurt shop, say your last employer was always "talkin' shit about frozen yogurt."

QUESTION:
"Have you ever been convicted of a felony?"

You don't want to sound scary here, but you also don't want to come off as a rube. Just say, "Convicted?"

QUESTION:
"When can you start work?"

Try to clear your schedule for that day so you can say "Right now." Employers love that. A trick I've also done is to start tidying up the area around the interview table, flipping over the chairs to oil the castors, then answering with, "I've already started!"

FOLLOWING UP

This is the often overlooked step in the interview process that can really separate you from the herd. Sending a note or email thanking your interviewer for his time is a courteous and appreciated gesture, but other top-tier applicants might think of doing that, too. Instead, go the extra mile, or more specifically, the number of miles it takes to go to the interviewer's house with a "Thank You!" ice cream cake and an oversized balloon that reads "I APPRECIATED YOU TAKING THE TIME TO MEET WITH ME!" Of course, you can't just leave an ice cream cake on somebody's front porch. It might melt. So break into the interviewer's house and put it

THE FOLLOW-UP

in his freezer. Then hide in the bushes till he gets home so you can tell him, "It's in your freezer." Now get out there and show your future employer that can-do spirit! JAMBA!

EPILOGUE

If you don't get the job after the interview, disguise yourself and go back in right away. The disguise can be as complicated as latex prosthetics, or as simple as carving your face up with a broken bottle. The important thing is, get back on that horse! ★

It's important to me that you, the reader, get a fair and balanced view of this great nation. In my last book,[16] I invited Average Americans from all walks of life to agree with me. In retrospect, that seems unfair to you, the purchaser. You paid for the opinions of Stephen Colbert, not some nobody like you. So this time other people will still get their say, but I'll be saying it.

MY TURN

BY: *Paul Delspinero*
Unemployed
Ardmore, Pennsylvania

Why am I smiling? Well, for starters, it's a Tuesday afternoon and I am high out of my gourd. Gourd. That's a weird word, right? Gourd. Gourd. Now it doesn't even sound like anything anymore. Secondly, I'm super high. Wait, did I already say that? But thirdly and most importantly, I'm ecstatic because I'm one of the 12.8 million Americans who are currently UNEMPLOYED.

And it is the best gig going. Oh sure, I could be a productive member of society and work to strengthen our economy and blah blah blah, but why bother when I've got a sugar daddy like Uncle Sam paying me to sit on my ass. Well, technically not sit--I'm actually laying down so I can play this great game where I try to toss Peanut M&Ms into my belly button.

I used to be like you, a working-stiff, slaving 40 hours a week at a soul suckin' B.S. job just so I could have lame things like "self worth" and "a place to go in the morning." Luckily, in the midst of the Recession, my boss Ted called me into his office and said:

"Paul, you've been one of our most trusted assistant managers for over a month, but we gotta lay you off."

So I said, "But Ted, I'm 34 with a salt water aquarium to take care of! If you fire me, I'LL TELL EVERYONE ABOUT YOUR AFFAIR WITH KAREN!"

Then Ted said, "Who's Karen?"

FROM DOWNTOOOOOWN!

[16] *I AM AMERICA (AND SO CAN YOU!)*—I can't believe I had to remind you.

Okay, Ted had me there. It was a long-shot that A) he was having an affair and B) it was with someone named Karen. I should've gone with "Jen."

Anyway, Ted gave me some paperwork about unemployment benefits and the rest is history, including the part where I stole 4 surge protectors on my way out of the building.

But readers, that layoff was <u>by far</u> the best thing that ever happened to me. Even better than the time I fist-bumped Brian Dennehy at the Pittsburgh airport. Super nice guy.

These government rubes make it so easy to pick the taxpayer pocket. All I gotta do is fill out a piddly unemployment form, then go online once a week and <u>say</u> I'm looking for a job. They'll never know that I've only looked on the floor around my gaming command lounger.

Then presto-casho, Big Government sends me a check for 300 bucks. <u>Every single week for 99 weeks</u>. Longest gig I've ever had.

GUILTY!

And I also get an additional $5 each week because I've declared my Yellow Tang a dependent.

So next time you're paying your taxes, chump, I want you to think of me, ol' Paul Delspinero, sucking your paycheck dry so I can stay home and rub one out to Judge Judy.

HEALTHCARE

fig 21.3-D. STEPHEN COLBERT

CHAPTER THREE

HEALTHCARE

"GIVE ME LIBERTY, AND
MERCURY TO CURE MY SYPHILIS,
OR GIVE ME DEATH!"

—*Ben Franklin, Paris, 1778*

Dr. Franklin was right. America does have the greatest healthcare system in the world. And the reason is simple: because America spends twice as much on healthcare per capita as any other country. Whatever is most expensive is always the best. Same reason the best Broadway show is *Spider-Man: The Musical* and the best house pet is a snow leopard. And our great healthcare is everywhere.

LOVES KIDS!

Just look around at America's endless bounty of hospitals, teeth-whitening centers, and nighttime dramas where young attractive doctors tongue each other in the supply closet.

We also have the most advanced care in the world. In my suburb, you can't swing a dead cat without hitting an MRI clinic. I've tried. They scanned the cat.[1] Turns out, it died from early-onset swinging. Why isn't someone working on a cure?!

Now critics love to point out that the American life expectancy of 78 ranks 42nd in the world. But that's ignoring the current Life Exchange Rate: 1 year in America is worth 10 in some foreign hellhole.

FARIDA MALHOTRA
BORN AUGUST 14, 1994
FRESHMAN AT
UC-CALCUTTA
GO FIGHTIN' LEPERS!

---

[1] Not with a Cat Scan—that would be ridiculous. MRI scans provide better clarity for soft tissue imaging, but use radio-frequency pulses rather than radiation. Do you really think I'd expose my dead cat to radiation for the sake of a pun? I'm not a monster.

Not only has American Healthcare always been the greatest, it has always been the firstest. U.S. doctors have always been medical pioneers. Sure, Germany has Wilhelm Conrad Röntgen who invented the X-ray; Scotland has Alexander Fleming who invented phlegm, and British obstetrician James Blundell performed the first-ever blood transfusion, from a kidney pie to Lord Byron.

SICK

But America has Robert Jarvik, who invented the artificial heart;[2] Jonas Salk, who invented polio; and Dr. John Woo, who in 1997 performed the first successful face transplant on Nicolas Cage and John Travolta. It was a medical marvel that grossed over 245 million dollars worldwide.

CURED

And let's not forget that it was physicians at R.J. Reynolds who discovered the T-Zone, and luckily they had already invented the product that relaxed it —Camel cigarettes.

And where can you find breast implants being inserted through the ear canal or regain lost years by injecting your face with ground-up monkey nut, or see the elderly sprinting down hospital halls with their new transplanted puma pelvis? Nowhere. But you can bet your bottom dollar we'll try it first.

As your doctor, I prescribe Smooth Flavor!

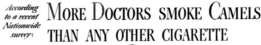

According to a recent Nationwide survey: MORE DOCTORS SMOKE CAMELS THAN ANY OTHER CIGARETTE

CAMELS *Costlier Tobaccos*

THANKS, DOC! GOT ANY HEROIN FOR MY ECZEMA?

---

[2] Sadly, too late to save The Tin Man.

But most impressive of all, America's E.R. doctors lead the globe in removing objects accidentally lodged in the rectum.

So that's American healthcare, and I'm just as opposed to "fixing" it as I am to "fixing" my dog. But some people want to cut off our healthcare's balls with a little plan called:

OBAMACARE:
HEALTHCARE OR HELL-TH-SCARE?

Book Nation, I can't predict what will happen after I turn in this manuscript. In fact, I can't even predict whether I'll turn it in at all. Discovery has been running a *Swamp Loggers* marathon, and it's really cutting into my writing time.[3]

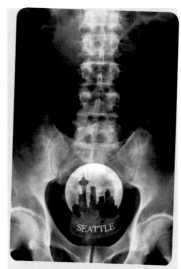

IF YOU **MUST** KNOW, I TRIPPED AND FELL WHILE VACATIONING IN THE PACIFIC NORTHWEST

So by the time you read this I don't know whether Obamacare will have been struck down by the Supreme Court. But if you *are* reading this, it probably means you're not dead,[4] which means you haven't been forced to submit to Obamacare.

THIS IS A JOBS PLAN?

And thank heavens for that. Because as we all know, Obamacare is a Trojan Horse, which refers to the Trojans for horses that it would pay for with your tax dollars. And since they're horses, we're talking the more expensive Trojan Magnums. That's right—Barack Obama wants to give Seabiscuit premium love gloves on the taxpayer dime! No wonder China is beating us at math.

Let's consider some arguments against Obamacare, and then, to be evenhanded, some other arguments against Obamacare.

First and foremost, Americans can already get any medical treatment we want, if we're willing to siphon enough money from the kids' college fund to pay for it.

Second and fifthmost, **SOCIALIZED MEDICINE DOESN'T WORK**.[5] Availability always

---

[3] Logs! From Swamps! The possibilities are endless!

[4] Or you're a very literate zombie, in which case—Back, fiend! I have fire!

[5] SOMETIMES MY CAPS LOCK KEY DOESN"T WORK EITHER.

opens the door to waste and abuse. Think about it—if they're free, who wouldn't get a bone marrow transplant? One of the reasons our healthcare is the best in the world is because it's exclusive. Right now, 50 million Americans are uninsured. Comprehensive coverage is reserved for the elite, like air travel in the 1960s. But look what happened when they let *everyone* fly. Airports became bus stations, mobbed with sweatpantsed Americans. Mark my word, you give everybody insurance and within a year gynecologist stirrups will have half the legroom.

Next thing you know, you'll be getting your colonoscopy at the DMV. It takes forever, and your colon always looks awful in the picture.

SMILE!

What's more, **IF GOVERNMENT CAN'T RUN ANYWHERE ELSE, WHY SHOULD WE THINK IT CAN RUN HEALTHCARE?** Do you really want Congress holding televised public hearings about your rectal bleeding and then issuing a 1,000-page advisory report about your anal polyps, while the prescription for your stool softener gets held up in committee?

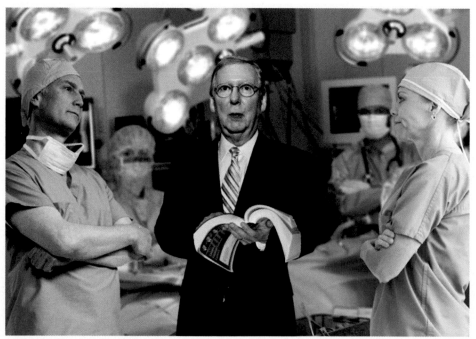

FILIBUSTERING YOUR ANAL FISTULA

Besides, **THE HEALTHCARE SYSTEM WORKS PERFECTLY AS IT IS, SO WHY CHANGE IT?!** Take the time I broke my wrist. The system worked. My driver took me to the nearest emergency room, and then to a different emergency room because the people in the first one looked kind of scary.[6] The hospital staff whisked me into a private suite and the doctor saw me immediately. The entire process of being X-rayed, getting my cast, posing for pictures with the staff and signing autographs took one hour.[7] Tell me: what about that needs fixing?

Frankly, **OBAMACARE IS NOTHING MORE THAN A SOCIALIST SCAM TO REDISTRIBUTE AMERICA'S WEALTH.** It will cause Joe and Jane Citizen to pay more taxes, Sam and Susan Small Business Owner to lay out a fortune in employee benefits, and Otis and Olivia Old

THIS IS JUST A TEST TO SEE WHETHER YOU CAN BE DISTRACTED FROM MY IMPORTANT MESSAGE TO THE LEFT. YOU FAILED.

Person to lose precious Medicare funding, which will then be funneled to pay for Ivan and Isabel Illegals when they pop out their Anchor Babies.[8] I don't want my tax dollars making it easier for the poor to have more children! Or fewer children! Why should I subsidize some teenager's birth control pills? Government has no business dictating family size. That's the Church's job.

Robbing Pop-Pop to pay Pedro doesn't even make medical sense. The vast bulk of medical care goes to people over the age of 80. The poor don't even live long enough to use it!

Worst of all, **OBAMACARE MEANS YOU CAN NO LONGER GO TO YOUR OWN DOCTOR**; now you have to go to one *assigned to you by the government.* So say goodbye to kindly old Doc Johnson, with his smiling eyes and his playful chuckle when he says "Bend over." Instead, you'll be going to Dr. Salaam Al-Quacki, in a clinic he runs out of an abandoned shipping container, who will secretly tally up what's wrong with you, so he can figure out which health internment facility to send you to: a Government Fatso Starvation Camp, or a Government Cigarette Smoker Reformatory, or a Government Frequent Farter Re-Education Center, or, if you have erectile dysfunction, a Penile Penal Colony. Why? Because **FEDERAL**

---

[6] NOT Black!

[7] It would've been less, but my assistant got writer's cramp.

[8] Alberto and Angela!

HEALTHCARE WILL DICTATE OUR LIFESTYLES. So if Dr. Hummus Breath determines that you are a threat to America's gene pool, *wham*—you're whisked off in a black Medevac helicopter. No thank you, Mr. President. I prefer to have my scrotum cupped by the Free Market.[9]

Point is, **OBAMACARE WILL DICTATE WHO LIVES AND WHO DIES.** I mean, we've all heard about the death panels that will decide whether or not Grandma is so sick that she'll be "sent to a farm upstate." (I'm being delicate to spare my younger readers, but I'm talking about killing her.) For more information click **HERE**![10]

Now some say, why not at least give Obamacare a try? What would that hurt? Well, they say that those who don't learn history are destined to repeat History class, so it's worth remembering our Republic's failed experiments with socialized medicine in the past. Have we forgotten Andrew Jackson's Jacksoncare? During Old Hickory's administration, it didn't matter if you were visiting your pfysician for bilious humors or brain fever. The treatment was always the same: kill an Indian— which may be effective for dropsy, but has shown no clinical results for Scrivener's palsy!

So sorry, Mr. President, but you can have my puzzlingly persistent heat rash when you pry it from between my warm, moist ass cheeks.

Back when our grandparents went to the town doctor, they just paid him with a chicken. No third party got in the way. I say we must return to this simpler time. Of course, when chickens become our currency, giving a doctor a sick chicken is like handing him a bad check. So, obviously, we're going to have to institute universal healthcare for chickens—Comprehensive nest to-platter coverage: vaccinations, prescription drug, optical, dental care, dry-rub. Because nothing is too good for our citizens' form of payment.

LEGAL AND TENDER

TERRIBLE TWOS

And if you had any doubt about the dangers of universal healthcare, look no further than its history. The first country to implement government healthcare was Germany in 1883 as a result of German Chancellor Otto Von Bismarck's social legislation. Well, just 6 years later, a government OBGYN delivered a 7-lb., 8-oz. Führer. Call me crazy, but I don't think the Greatest Generation should have to pay for Baby Adolf's wellness care.

---

[9] The Invisible Hand is suprisingly well-moisturized.

[10] Did it work? **YES NO**

Still think Socialized Medicine is "all that?" Well, let's ask an actual Canadian. I have no trouble imagining what he would say.

MY TURN

BY: Gordon Lloyd McKenzie-King

Canadian

Well, hello! How the heck are ya? And the family as well? Super. Bit of unseasonable weather, eh? Hope you didn't catch the bug that's going around. If you're feeling sniffly, I'd love to bring over some hot maple soup. It's got oouddles of flavour.

(Sourry for my superfluouus Canadian u's in words like "flavour" and "colour." Up here you gotta layer in the extra vowels to keep the consonants warm.)

Anyways, it's my pleasure to help a friend from south of the ol' 49th. 'Cause far as I understand it, when you Americans get sick, your options are soup, paying thousands for health insurance, or your government letting you die in the street like a doug. Sourry, "dog."

Figure 6: Dog

Canada has the best darn healthcare system in the world. Of course, that's just my two loonies, or if you'd prefer, one toonie. Which as I write, is worth just a bit more than your two dollars. Could be that's 'cause America spends more on healthcare than Canada spends on catsup-flavored

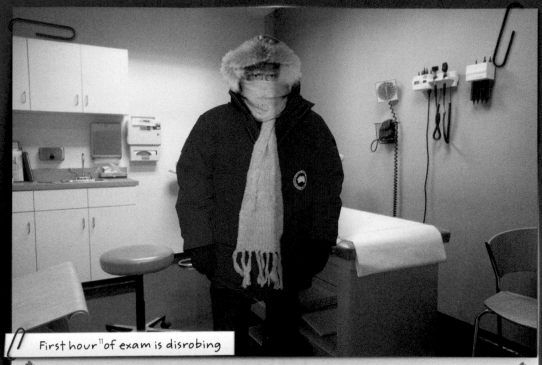

First hour[11] of exam is disrobing

potato crispers and Junior AAA Pond Hockey League tickets combined. Yet it still has worse health outcomes? Heck if I knouw why.

See, up here in the Great Healthy North, we believe in doing things fair. We see healthcare as a right every Canadian deserves, just like a government-issued photo of the Queen.

Constitutionally, She could dissolve our Parliament in a heartbeat and enslave us all in Her wig powder mines, but She's too proper. And thanks to Her Majesty, every Canadian regardless of colour, creed, or religioun, has access to free, high-quality medical care.

Handsome Woman, eh?

Now, a lot of folks in the States have funny ideas about our system. For instance, we don't "ration" medicine. We share it. No Canadian is ever denied access to care. Unless the Conseil National de Poids et Mesures says that Saskatchewan's MRI machine must be shut down for re-greasing with poutine. But that only happens between Boxing Day and Canadian New Year's Eve (May 17th).

[11] Metric Hour!

It's been a while since I've apologized. Sourry.

Now, before you see the doc, you have to fill out a few forms. The first is your standard Smalltalk Questionnaire-- 22 pages asking after your mother, whether you'd like a cup of cocoa, if anyone has offered to hang up your coat, etc. Then you move on to the forms in the Healthcare Application Binder that the government mails out the first Tuesday and third Thursday of every even-numbered month. Make sure yours is up to date, eh, or you'll have to fill out a Healthcare Application Binder Application Binder for a new one! And that can take a bit.

When that's all done, you grab a number and wait on the wooden Medical Bench until you're called to hand your forms to the Reception Clerk, who distributes them to the Royal Mounted Check-Up Schedulers, who fax them to the Provincial Bureau of Health Processing. From there, it's a short portage along the St. Lawrence for the Postal Canoe to deliver your appointment date.

Of course, as citizens of a bilingual nation, Canadians receive medical care in both English and French. Not bad, eh? Sourry.[12]

Now, in certain cases, there can be a short wait. For instance, in the Provinces, first priority for medical attention always goes to members of our noble First Nations.

But if you're feeling so darn sick you absolutely must see the doc right away, we Canadians have an answer for that, too. We go to America and pay for the best darn treatment in the wourld!

First In Line for Dewlap Tuck

Well, thanks for listening. Sourry to take off, but I gotta drive my son's hockey troupe on a field trip to the Michael Bublé Museum. See you later, eh?

Sourry!

[12] Je suis désolé, eh?

STOP, DROP, ENROLL

So, I've proven to my satisfaction that this is the greatest healthcare system in the world. That said, it's no cake walk—which is good since a lot of you can't walk due to all that cake. Besides, Americans love a challenge. And health insurance companies generously make their enrollment forms as difficult as possible to help take your mind off your ailment. To prepare you for the real thing, I've included a sample insurance form as a dry run.[13]

PLEASE
DO NOT
STAPLE IN
THIS AREA

PRESCOTT MEDICAL CORP
MEDICARE DMERC OPERATIONS
P O BOX 123456
BUTTERNUT ID 12344567

HEALTH INSURANCE CLAIM FORM

SUBSCRIBER INFORMATION

NAME:

(LAST NAME)   (FIRST NAME)

(INSURANCE NAME: It's like your porn name. Combine your childhood pet's name with the disease you least want to die from. *Example: Whiskers Ebola.*)

HOME ADDRESS (PLEASE FILL OUT IN MORSE CODE):

TELEPHONE (USE SPACE PROVIDED):
Enter it here ❏

SOCIAL SECURITY NUMBER (FOR EACH DIGIT, ROUND UP):
❏❏❏ – ❏❏ – ❏❏❏❏

OCCUPATION: (SELECT THE ONE CLOSEST TO YOUR JOB)

❏ Ship Captain
❏ Dog Whisperer
❏ Homicidal Clown
❏ Articulated welding robot

❏ Robert Mugabe Henchman
❏ Duchess of Cambridge
❏ Cockney Infomercial Pitchman
❏ Asian

SEX:
❏ Male
❏ Female
❏ Hoping the doctor can nail that one down

REASON FOR ENROLLMENT:

❏ New enrollment
❏ Add dependent to existing plan
❏ Want to be drain on small business owners
❏ Afraid of catching a teeny-tiny cold because I'm a coward

---

[13] By the way, if you have the dry runs, you're gonna need to list it as a pre-existing condition.

CHOOSE DESIRED PLAN TYPE:

- ❏ HMO
- ❏ PPO
- ❏ MLB
- ❏ KFC
- ❏ JFK, BLOWN AWAY, WHAT ELSE DO I HAVE TO SAY?

DID YOU START THE FIRE?

- ❏ I did
- ❏ I did not

DEPENDENTS COVERED

Dependents? Wow, sounds like your family may be a little too reliant on you. Shouldn't you teach them some self-sufficiency? What if their car breaks down and they're forced to survive in the woods? They won't be able to because you've done everything for them! Your son will say, "I guess I'll just run and jump in a wolf's mouth because my father never taught me how to be independent." Besides, are you sure those are your dependents? Am I the only one who thinks that Billy looks a lot like the guy who put in your storm windows?

_____
_____
_____
_____

HEALTH HISTORY

In the past 110 years, has any person listed on this enrollment form consulted a healthcare provider, received treatment, or been hospitalized for any of the following conditions or diseases. This will help us determine your pre-existing conditions. *(Note: If enrollee is not yet 110 years old, please wait until such time to fill out this form.)*

IMPORTANT! PLEASE GIVE COMPLETE DETAILS OF EACH "YES" ANSWER ON THE "ADDITIONAL MEDICAL DETAILS" PAGE, WHICH HAS BEEN HIDDEN IN RANDOM, SPECIALLY MARKED BOXES OF HONEY NUT CHEERIOS.

NOSE/EYES/EARS/THROAT DISORDERS:

A. Can you breathe? Has this been a recurring problem?

❏ Yes ❏ No

B. Can you smell properly? Scratch and sniff this question: Does it smell like Chicken Teriyaki?

❏ Yes ❏ Sesame Chicken

C. Do you have trouble reading this?

❏ Yes ❏ No

D. Do your tear ducts secrete uncontrollably when you watch *Old Yeller*?

❏ Yes ❏ No

E. If yes, have you ever been diagnosed as a big gaywad?

❏ Yes

F. Please indicate which number you see in the diagram below:

- ❏ 66
- ❏ 43
- ❏ Slibbidy Five
- ❏ Can't see number, only cackling demon

SKIN CONDITIONS/DISORDERS:

A. Do you have acne, birthmarks, dermatitis, eczema, psoriasis, skin, sweat glands, or body hair?
❏ Yes ❏ No

B. What classic American foodstuff is your skin most like?
❏ a pie crust
❏ a brick of room temperature cheddar
❏ cooling top layer of day-old pudding
❏ McNugget

C. It's 2 a.m., you're drunk, you're the only other person at the bar. Do you sleep with you?
❏ Yes ❏ Was it Tequila?

D. Does your hair continue to grow during a full moon? If so, please, make sure you're not a werewolf by shooting yourself in the heart with a silver bullet.
❏ Yes ❏ No

E. What method do you use to remove body hair?
❏ Razor with 4+ blades
❏ Stress
❏ Brazilian thatch-wrangler

F. Does your skin have a dark pigmentation, which makes it hard to get approved for bank loans?
❏ No
❏ Currently getting pulled over by cops

BRAIN/NERVOUS SYSTEM CONDITIONS/DISORDERS:

A. Do you hear voices coming from inanimate objects, like your radio or car GPS unit?
❏ Yes ❏ No

B. Do you have feelings of déjà vu? ❏ Yes ❏ No

C. Parlez-vous français? ❏ Oui ❏ No

B. Do you have feelings of déjà vu? ❏ Yes ❏ No

D. Have you ever undergone a partial lobotomy?
❏ No ❏ Pancakes

RESPIRATORY CONDITIONS/DISORDERS:

A. Do you experience shortness of breath when climbing a mountain or running a marathon or running a marathon up a mountain?
❏ Yes ❏ No ❏ Can't talk right now

B. Is neumonia spelled right here? Our spell check is broken.
❏ Yes ❏ Pno

C. When you cough or wheeze, what animal do you most sound like?
(Please include sample of animal for comparison)

MUSCULOSKELETAL CONDITIONS/DISORDERS:

A. Is there a scary skeleton living inside you?
❏ Yes ❏ No

B. Do you have any muscles whatsoever? If so, are you juicing? Please include a year's worth of urine.
❏ Yes ❏ No

C. Please choose your approximate skull shape.

❏ Caucasoid Thief   ❏ Negroid Murderer

❏ Irish Landsquatter   ❏ Bloodthirsty Aztec

❏ Mongol Occultist   ❏ American

D. Did the King of Pop ever offer to buy your bones?
❏ Yes ❏ No

E. If you smash your funny bone against something, is it funny?
❏ No ❏ Why do they call it that?

DIGESTIVE CONDITIONS/DISORDERS:

A. Do you have any problems with digestion? Eat this form and monitor the amount of time it takes to poop it out.   ❏ Yes ❏ No

B. Have you experienced rectal bleeding? ❏ Yes ❏ No
B1. If yes, do you remember why? ❏ I don't think I… ❏ Oh, God.

C. Which of the following do you do regularly?
❏ Have bowel movements ❏ Drop the kids off at the pool ❏ Take the Browns to the Super Bowl
❏ Butt yodel in the Toilet Canyon ❏ Give Osama Brown Laden a burial at sea

URINARY CONDITIONS/DISORDERS:

A. Does it hurt when you pee? ❏ Yes ❏ No
B. Does it hurt others when you pee? ❏ Yes ❏ No

HEART AND CIRCULATORY CONDITIONS/DISORDERS:

A. Do you have a persistent pounding in your chest?
   ❏ Yes ❏ No
B. Have you had this affliction your entire life?
   ❏ Yes ❏ No
C. Sounds like your heart could be loose. Try
   tightening it by twisting your nipples really hard.
   ❏ Yes ❏ No
D. If I prick you, do you not bleed?
   ❏ Forsooth ❏ 'Ods Bodkins
E. Do you engage in a minimum of 30 minutes of
   cardiovascular exercise, at least 3 days a week?
   ❏ No ❏ LIAR!!!!
F. Are you currently suffering from a broken heart?
   ❏ Yes ❏ No
G. If yes, was it Jenny? Did she do this to you?
   We told you to stay away from her, Michael!
   ❏ Yes ❏ No
H. Have you ever received a baboon
   heart transplant?
   ❏ No ❏

FEMALE REPRODUCTIVE:

A. Has God ever punished you with the Time of the
   Blood?
   ❏ Yes ❏ No
B. After you went into the tent for six days then
   cleansed with a ritual bath, what offering did you
   present the High Priest?
   ❏ Two turtledoves
   ❏ An unblemished calf
   ❏ Still hiding in shame
C. Is, uh, the stuff, pertaining to the—ahem—all okay
   and whatnot?
   ❏ Yes ❏ No
D. What about the outer-type things—are those, um,
   are they…uh…God…
   ❏ What? ❏ Just spit it out!
E. Is Aunt Flo in town?
   ❏ Yes ❏ No
F. Are you pregnant?
   ❏ Yes ❏ No
G. If yes, how far along are you?
   ❏ 1 to 3 months
   ❏ 4 to 7 months
   ❏ 8 to 16 months (am pilot whale)

MALE REPRODUCTIVE:

A. Do you have any sexual transmitted diseases?
   ❏ Yes ❏ Was it Jenny?
B. Does the idea of a lady blacksmith turn you on?
   ❏ Yes ❏ No
C. Really? Imagine her forging a sword with her
   strong but supple hands.
   ❏ Yes ❏ No
D. Okay, let's say you're a knight. You've been
   crusading for three years with what you thought
   was your young squire blacksmith. Until one day,
   you've made camp by a river. And you woke
   up earlier than usual to engage in your morning
   ablutions, only to find what you thought was
   young Geoffrey of York, lost in the sensual
   pleasure of a mountain stream cascading down
   his full proud snow-white breasts. Come on, is
   that not hot to you at all?
   ❏ Yes ❏ I pity you.
E. How large is your prostate?
   Please round up to the nearest fruit.
   ❏ Currant
   ❏ Bing cherry
   ❏ Japanese plum
   ❏ Dosc pear
   ❏ Beefsteak tomato
   ❏ Muskmelon
F. Have you ever engaged in
   any homosexual activity?
   ❏ Yes ❏ No
G. How about gay stuff?
   ❏ Yes ❏ No
H. Not supergay. I'm talking about, like, at camp.
   Come on—nothing to be ashamed of.
   We've all been there.
   ❏ Yes ❏ No
I. I mean, some places in Europe,
   men walk arm-in-arm all the time.
   Means nothing.
   ❏ Yes ❏ No
J. Are you sure? I won't tell anyone.
   ❏ Yes
K. I knew it!
L. Please trace your genitals in the space provided.
   Just press them against this sheet and trace away. If
   you need more room, well, congratulations, buddy.

MENTAL AND BEHAVIORAL:

A. Are you still thinking about the lady blacksmith? ❏ Yes ❏ C'mon!

B. Have you ever considered bulimia, Fatty? ❏ Yes ❏ No

C. Do you suffer from delusions, including the one where check-boxes appear as wolves?

  ❏ Yes

D. Have you ever suffered from Tourette's Syndrome? ❏ Asshole ❏ Cock Burger

E. Draw the shape I'm thinking of:

F. BOO! Did you jump?

  ❏ Yes ❏ BOO! How about now? ❏ Yes ❏ BOO! Now?

G. Have you ever been diagnosed with a mental BOOOO!!!!! Got you that time, right?

  ❏ Yes ❏ No

H. Are you currently on any antidepressants?

  ❏ Does it really matter? ❏ Going to take a nap

I. Let's play a little random association game. I'll say a word, and you tell me the first thing you think of. Okay, here goes: Tulips.

  ❏ Murdering small animals

J. Have you ever experienced delusions of grandeur, like thinking you could get health insurance?

  ❏ Yes ❏ No

What do you think these boxes mean?
Failure to fill out or check the appropriate box(es) may delay your application.

❏❏❏-❏-❏❏❏❏   ❏❏❏❏❏❏❏
"❏❏❏❏❏❏❏ ❏❏❏❏"   ❏❏❏❏!
❏❏❏❏❏❏❏
❏❏❏❏❏❏❏❏❏❏❏,
❏❏❏❏❏❏❏❏❏.❏❏❏❏

LEAVE THIS SPACE BLANK. THE ACCOUNT EXECUTIVE WILL NEED IT TO FACTOR YOUR SCORE.

PREVIOUS PHYSICIANS:
Please list the regular physician or medical care practitioner for each proposed recipient.
Provide the date last seen, the reason, and their height in furlongs.

Primary: _____

_____

Do you find Dr. Quinn Medicine Woman attractive?
❏ Yes ❏ No

Oh, a medicine woman is fine, but a lady blacksmith is weird. You need to look in the mirror.

AUTHORIZATION:

By signing here, I waive any and all rights to privacy. I agree that my medical history and personal information may be drunk-tweeted at 3 in the morning, written on the wall of a food court bathroom, or posted on Craigslist under the heading "SBM seeking Open-Minded Albino for Light Role-play."

I understand that if my signature/date do not appear and/or are not current, my enrollment will be declined.

DO NOT SIGN HERE   DATE OF MOON LANDING

_____   _____

PHARMACEUTICALS:

Yes, there's a pill for that!

Nothing makes me happier and more proud to be an American than our pharmaceutical industry. Also, nothing makes me dizzier and more prone to nausea, dry mouth, vertigo, and night terrors. I shudder to think where we'd be without the wide variety of prescription drugs to treat our think-shuddering.

Now, there are those who insist that the pharmaceutical industry puts profits over helping the sick. But the truth is, companies like Merck, Pfizer, AstraZeneca, Eli Lilly, Novartis, Bristol-Meyers Squibb, and Los Carteles del Juarez Medicinales spend millions of dollars coming up with new cures for our crippling diseases. And they spend even more to come up with cures to treat their previous treatments.[15]

ISN'T IT TIME YOU STARED INTO THE MIDDLE DISTANCE WITH A PALPABLE SENSE OF RELIEF?

But in a true show of American innovation, the industry isn't content to cure diseases that currently exist. Their dedicated team of Pharmagineers™ are hard at work coming up with new maladies you may or may not have.[16] For example, in the past, kicking your spouse repeatedly during the night just meant you were getting out resentment built up over the course of a marriage. Now it's "Restless Leg Syndrome."

REMEMBER...

PILLS AREN'T THE ANSWER TO EVERY PROBLEM. SOMETIMES IT'S SUPPOSITORIES.

Perhaps you have one of those jobs where you work all night, and sometimes find yourself nodding off. You may have Shift Work Sleep Disorder (SWSD), characterized by sleepiness, insomnia, and difficulty concentrating on the job. Yes, sleepiness and insomnia are both

---

[14] They didn't.

[15] "That Which Does Not Kill You Makes You A Repeat Customer."

[16] Spoiler Alert: You have them!

symptoms, so don't try and pretend you don't have it. SWSD is totally different from simply being tired, and if you've been laboring under the misconception that you're just exhausted, that only shows what a bad case of SWSD you have—you're not thinking straight!

But the pharmaceutical industry knows that the best drugs in the world mean nothing if they don't get to the people who are persuaded to need them. That's why most companies spend twice as much on the marketing of drugs as they do on research and development.

PROMOTIONAL PENS *through* **THE AGES**

The American pharmaceutical industry has been at the forefront of cutting edge advancements in marketing that have improved the lives of millions of sales reps, advertising execs, and customized pen manufacturers.

1797 AGUE? TRY LEECHES

1888 Yellow Fever? Reach for Dr. Parker's Leech Elixir

2012 SOMETHING? ASK YOUR DOCTOR ABOUT Leechbutrin™

But some doctors, uninterested in advancing the cause of science, stick to well-tested drugs proven effective for well-documented illnesses. That's why drug companies advertise to consumers directly, so they can pester their doctors into a prescription.

In fact, a drug's marketing is all you need to know before deciding whether or not it's right for you. Are you a black-and-white outline of a depressed woman walking in a sunny field? Try Cymbalta. Do you like throwing footballs through large, suggestive tire swings? Give Levitra a shot! Were you once The Flying Nun? Did you date Burt Reynolds? Boniva is for you![17]

EVIDENCE OF EARLY BONE DAMAGE

---

[17] Are you currently Burt Reynolds? See previous line about Levitra!

POPULAR AMERICAN DRUGS

VIAGRA® (SILDENAFIL CITRATE)

Can you hear the drums of victory heralding the triumph that is Viagra? Well you should, because beating those drums are the rock hard phalluses of 72-year-old men. To those who would say a pill that has given millions of men recreational California redwood and raked in billions in profits isn't the greatest achievement in scientific history, let me just say I can't hear you because all the blood that was keeping my brain moist has plunged into my shaft. If Viagra wasn't the most important drug ever invented, why would so many Indian and Mexican basement pharmaceutical labs spend countless hours mixing Tylenol, Similac, and Pine-Sol into a non-prescription knockoff that you can buy over the Internet? You don't see an entire industry built around producing black market forms of Claritin. Seven billion weekly spam messages from Canadian pharmacies aren't advertising great deals on Neosporin that will GIVE YOUR LADY MUCH SATISFY ON THE SEX TIME SHE WANT SO BAD IN ALL HAPPY SPOTS.[18]

LET'S KNOCK ORTHOPEDIC BOOTS!

CIALIS® (TADALAFIL[19])

Cialis is similar to Viagra, except that it is made exclusively for sex while watching the sunset in adjacent outdoor bathtubs. Cialis is to be used only under these conditions, and only by heterosexual couples aged 48 and over. Any attempt to increase blood flow to the penises of homosexuals enjoying fall foliage in side-by-side outdoor shower stalls or teenagers observing the aurora borealis in adjoining open-air steam rooms will neutralize the active ingredient.

[20]

RITALIN® (METHYLPHENIDATE)

A psycho-stimulant drug commonly used to treat attention deficit disorder, youthful displays of exuberance, joyful bursts of curiosity, prolonged wonderment, and persistent enthusiasm. Symptoms of a patient in need of Ritalin include trouble focusing, sudden mood swings, and being a child.

AMBIEN® (ZOLPIDEM)

Ambien is prescribed to treat insomnia. It is a fantastic drug to have when you can't sleep due to your anxiety about how many prescription drugs you're taking. Some people also report incidences of sleepwalking under the influence of Ambien. People have driven their cars, cooked and eaten food, and even had sex while sleeping, only to wake with no recollection of their actions. I'm guessing there's at least one guy who's had sex with food in his car, and wisely chose not to report it.

---

[18] ***NOW BONUS TURGID MANHOOD, PURCHASE V1A8RA NOW! ***

[19] *Tadalafil* is named for what you shout when the drug takes effect.

[20] Quick Question: What is happening here? Are they getting clean *before or after* the dirty business? God, I hope it's before.

FLOMAX® (TAMSULOSIN)

If you're like me, you spend a lot of time with your silver-haired buddies yachting, golfing, biking, kaya-king, and aging. And when you're out with the boys, there is nothing more embarrassing than having to urinate. Not only are you forced to suffer the humiliating nicknames—Pee-Pee Herman, Urethra Franklin, Flowra Faucet Sprayjors—but you could miss out on the memorable moments, like when Preston finally puts away enough Johnnie Blue to tell Art he's been taking his wife Cynthia behind the pool shed after couples brunch for the past nine years.

Flomax treats urinary symptoms like hesitation, extreme urgency, and dribbling, which to be fair, would make your penis an unstoppable point guard—especially with your basketball-sized prostate easily within reach.

DO YOU SUFFER FROM AN OVERACTIVE BLADDER?

HOW ABOUT NOW?

NOW?

XANAX® (ALPRAZOLAM)

Xanax is an anti-anxiety drug that calms people down in a number of ways. One, it enhances the effects of the neurotransmitter gamma-aminobutyric acid. Two, it has a name that you can spell forward or backwards—one less thing to worry about.

Xanax is in a class of medications called benzo-diazepines, whose primary application is alleviating symptoms associated with human life. Those suffering with this condition often experience prolonged periods of anxiety, painful memories, and extreme fear. In longtime sufferers of human consciousness, severe panic, insomnia, and regrets so acute they are palpable in the chest are also common. If you see your doctor with these symptoms, he may prescribe Xanax. Higher doses are recommended for those experiencing time slipping, sieve-like, through their fingers, loss of spiritual mooring in a cruel and arbitrary universe, and having children.

Should Xanax's mild amnesic effects cause you to forget to take a dose, do not panic. Instead, worry deeply. It is beyond your powers to change the past, but had you the courage to attend to the dimming heartbeat of your childhood aspirations as you aged, perhaps you would not be so estranged from the person you once were.

TAKE TWO XANAX EVERY FOUR HOURS TO TREAT THE INEXORABLE MARCH OF TIME

VICODIN®

(ACETAMINOPHEN/HYDROCODONE)

Here's a shocking statistic: 131.2 million Americans have a prescription for Vicodin. That's nearly half our population and 40% more than the next leading drug.[21] This can only mean one thing—Vicodin is America's best medicine. The invisible hand of the market has chosen, and it needs one quick for its chronic invisible wrist pain. Also, let's be honest, its invisible shoulder feels like it's got needles sticking into it, so maybe it should just say fuck it and take the 750 milligrams, because it knows if it takes the 500 it's just going to need another one in two hours since it went biking yesterday and no doubt its invisible knee is going to flare up, and because who is it kidding, Scotch just ain't cuttin' it anymore.

AIRBORNE® (HERBS, HOKUM, BUBBLES)

Ever wish you could take a supplement that boosts your immune system to fight off the common cold? Then Airborne may be right for you. Want to take a supplement that actually does that? Then Airborne may not be right for you. Created by an elementary school teacher, Airborne is most effective when used by those who approach medicine with the naïve wonder of a third grader. Also available by the generic name, Sweet Tarts.

NEXIUM®

(ESOMEPRAZOLE)

I'm not 100% sure on the science behind the drug, but based on the commercials, I believe it works by being purple.

BOTH MATRIX PILLS COMBINED!

According to a curious new study published in the *New England Journal of Publishing*, two out of every five readers will feel as though he or she has absorbed actual facts and figures, despite being given nothing more than a placebo sidebar completely devoid of any actual information.

---

[21] Which I believe treats Vicodin withdrawal.

MAKE YOUR OWN DRUG!

Creating a new wonder drug is a piece of cake. All it takes is a catchy drug name, a terrible sounding illness, a massive marketing budget, and a 10-sided die. If you do not own a 10-sided die, just contact your nearest Dungeons and Dragons player. If it's a Friday or Saturday night, do not worry—he will be home.[22]

Roll the die once for each of the columns below

DRUG NAME

PREFIX	SUFFIX
❶ PRILO	❶ MAX
❷ ZAXXA	❷ DRENE
❸ SKELA	❸ BUTRIN
❹ VAGI	❹ THX-1138
❺ SINGU	❺ VITRA
❻ MXYZPLTK	❻ CILLIN
❼ FLO	❼ EXPIALADOCIOUS
❽ ZYPRE	❽ BREX
❾ YABBADABBA	❾ IAGRA
❿ ORTHO	❿ PATRONUM

DRUG DELIVERY METHOD

APPEARANCE	FORM
❶ BLUE	❶ TABLET
❷ PURPLE	❷ LIQUID GEL-CAP
❸ RAZZLEBERRY	❸ SYRINGE
❹ INVISIBLE	❹ SUPPOSITORY
❺ CANTILEVERED	❺ SUPPOSITORY (CHEWABLE)
❻ BARBED	❻ NASAL SPRAY
❼ JACKSON-POLLOCK-ESQUE	❼ PRESCRIPTION BITE STICK
❽ SOUR CREAM & ONION	❽ GENEROUSLY APPLIED BALM
❾ MINTY	❾ FULL-BODY WRAP
❿ BAMM-BAMM SHAPED	❿ TRANQ DART

---

[22] Knock loudly—he's probably in the basement.

AILMENT

ADJECTIVE	BODY PART	CLASSIFICATION
1 RESTLESS	**1** EYE	**1** DISORDER
2 ENGORGED	**2** BLADDER	**2** SYNDROME
3 MALE PATTERN	**3** LUNG	**3** FEVER
4 DICKENSIAN	**4** ELBOW	**4** PLAGUE
5 JUGGLER'S	**5** SCROTUM	**5** SURPRISE
6 GREGARIOUS	**6** NOSTRIL	**6** MADNESS
7 RAPIDLY MULTIPLYING	**7** JAW	**7** ESQUIRE
8 INGROWN	**8** COLON	**8** SIMPLEX II
9 PHANTOM	**9** NIPPLE	**9** PHANTISIS
10 HOMOSEXUAL	**10** SKULL	**10** STIGMATA

COMMERCIAL

LOCATION	IMAGERY	ANIMATED EFFECT
1 SPRING MEADOW	**1** PARTING STORM CLOUDS	**1** SOOTHING BLUE ABDOMINAL GLOW
2 SUBURBAN LIVING ROOM	**2** WILD HORSE GALLOPING THROUGH GRASS	**2** CRANIAL THUNDERING
3 GOLF COURSE	**3** DANCING OVULATING WOMEN	**3** PULSATING RED CIRCLES
4 SCREAMING KID'S PARTY	**4** SUGGESTIVE MOTORCYCLE REVVING	**4** EVIL, SCOWLING POLLEN CLUSTERS
5 STEEP HIKING TRAIL	**5** WYNONNA JUDD	**5** FOOT-INDUCED WILDFIRE
6 INTERIOR OF ASCENDING AORTA	**6** FOOTBALL BEING THROWN THROUGH VAGINA SUBSTITUTE[23]	**6** CGI TARTAR OGRES
7 WINDSWEPT BEACH	**7** RENOVATED CANOE	**7** SWELLING PURPLENESS
8 BOTTOM OF NURSING HOME STAIRS	**8** WRINKLED HANDS CLASPED IN UNCERTAINTY	**8** DEPRESSED, BOUNCING OVAL BEING
9 SEA OF PHLEGM	**9** HOBBLING MARIONETTE	**9** ANXIOUS, FLOATING WORDS
10 HEAVEN?	**10** AGREEABLE AFRICAN AMERICAN	**10** MELTING SINUS GOLEM

RECALLED DUE TO

1 CHOKING HAZARD	**5** INTERFERRING WITH RADIO TRANSMISSIONS	**8** INSPIRING ORIGINAL LIFETIME MOVIE
2 PENDING LAWSUITS	**6** *60 MINUTES* INVESTIGATIVE REPORT	**9** [CENSORED BY U.S. GOVERNMENT]
3 WHAT SOME ARE CALLING "VAPOR BONE"	**7** CAUSING NERVOUSNESS IN NEARBY LIVESTOCK	**10** WHAT WILL EVENTUALLY SEEM LIKE AN HILARIOUS MIX-UP
4 ANGERING POSEIDON		

---

[23] IMPORTANT: Do not use actual vagina.

ALTERNATIVE MEDICINE

The Complete Waste of Time and Money That You Should Really Give a Second Look

For every person with a Cadillac insurance policy like mine, there's a woman out there giving birth in the back of a Corolla, which wouldn't be so awful if those Japanese needed more legroom.[24] But while employers like me won't pay for health insurance,[25] I'm not going to do *nothing* for you. I'm gonna *suggest* things that do nothing for you.

Fear not: even if you can't afford the kind of medicine that works, you can probably afford the kind that sounds like it should work. It's what's known to people outside the scientific community as "alternative medicine," which is an abbreviation for "alternative *to* medicine."[26]

Here's a primer on some of the more popular folk remedies, dietary regimens, quasi-religious belief systems, and orifice powerwashing. They cost less because they do less, but more important, they cost less.

COLON HYDROTHERAPY

As they say, an ounce of prevention is worth a pound of cure. Then it stands to reason that 64-fluid-ounces of warm soapy water up your poopchute has got to do something.

The idea here is to keep your most important exit tube easy-breezy and smooth-movin' because the unmethodical way you usually go about that business just isn't cutting it.[27] Your body had millions of years to evolve a system of excreting waste, but now a stranger in Crocs and a rubber smock is taking over.

I don't want to get too technical here, but the process involves what

Try to relax.

DR. ROSEBUD
CERTIFIED COLONIC
IRRIGATIONIST

science describes as sticking a hose up your butt and filling you like a water balloon. While you lie on a table specially designed to present your hindquarters,[28] a machine flushes up to 20 gallons of water into your rectum in order to dislodge whatever's clinging to your lodge. It's like a New York City doorman spritzing down the sidewalk, only it involves less fecal matter. The therapist may also introduce a variety of enzymes, probiotics, herbs or coffee. Please indicate whether you take cream and sugar.[29]

---

[24] That's not racist, that's racial.

[25] Don't think of yourself as uninsured. Think of yourself as a healthcare daredevil.

[26] Just like "alternative music."

[27] Shit doesn't just happen.

[28] Advertised in the back of finer men's magazines.

[29] If they ask "one lump or two?"—GET OUT OF THERE!

Upon removal, you erupt like Mount Krap-atoa. Legend has it that through their tears first-time practitioners can see the purging of wads of gum, marbles, particularly hearty bread crusts, kale shrapnel, and cufflinks.[30]

Is it effective? Well, we know that the worse a medicine tastes, the better it is for you. Of course, if you taste any medicine here, then they have the hose in too far. And considering that a high colonic is an almost unparalleled act of dehumanizing debasement—it's like being sodomized by Aquaman[31]—you know it must have worked!

CLEANSING Of course, there are other ways to flush out your digestive tract without Jet Skiing the wrong way up the old Erie Canal. There's cleansing, which combines all the fun of laxatives with the gnawing delirium of gradual starvation.

NETI POT An increasingly popular non-pharmaceutical cold remedy, the Neti Pot is a cute little creamer-looking teapot which is filled with a saline solution that is then poured through your nose.

LOOK! IT'S HELEN HUNT!

This is similar to Colon Hydrotherapy, though in this case the toxins are flushed out through the nostril, which is why the nose is often referred to as the "colon of the face." Neti pot use has recently been linked to several deaths caused by a brain-eating amoeba that lives in tap water, which is why you should only use a Neti pot with distilled water and also GIVE UP ON EVERYTHING BECAUSE, IN CASE YOU WEREN'T LISTENING, THERE IS A BRAIN-EATING AMOEBA IN TAP WATER.

CHROMOTHERAPY Different colors cure different things! Pocket as many paint swatches as you can from your local Sherwin Williams—it's free. For instance, Arctic Blue cures herpes, while Country Squire controls angina and Rustic Adobe will make short work of athlete's foot—one imagines.

EAR CANDLING This practice is based on the sound premise that human ears are the primary source of disease. You simply lie on your side with a lit hollow candle poked through a pie tin, then inserted into your ear canal, creating an updraft in the chimney of the candle that sucks out... I'm gonna say, toxins?... from the body. Now, folks in the Medical Establishment call Ear Candling "ineffective" and "dangerous,"[32] but I say that's reason enough to give it a try. Why are they so threatened by it? I found it almost unnervingly effective— I had no idea my head was clogged with so much candle wax! As soon as my hair grows back, I'm going to try this one again.

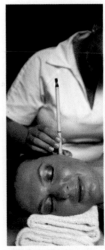

SURE...WHY NOT?

---

[30] It's always in the last place you look!

[31] For more information see *Dark Waters, Dark Truths: The Aqualad Story*, by Jackson Hyde.

[32] Expert tip: You can cut down the danger caused by ear candling by combining it with a high colonic. It's the perfect fit. There's a convenient water source right there! If your hair catches fire, you can put it out with your own high-pressure waste. (NOTE TO SELF: Patent ass candling? Check Internet. NOTE TO READERS: Do not check Internet!)

AROMATHERAPY Different smells cure different things! Here's a bargain tip: For just 20 bucks, you can pick up a fully stocked spice rack[33] at TJ Maxx.

CHIROPRACTIC MEDICINE Chiropractic medicine is an ancient, ageless practice that was founded in the 1890s and has grown into the third largest healthcare profession, behind medicine and any other form of medicine. Chiropractors make manual adjustments to the spine, combining the skill of massage with the technical precision of popping bubble wrap. Because of the delicate nature of the back, in the wrong hands, it's extremely dangerous. But in the right hands, it's merely dangerous.

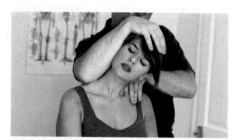

REMEMBER: THE HEALTHY NECK
SHOULD BE BANANA-SHAPED

CRYSTAL HEALING This mysterious practice has antecedents back to ancient times, from Mesoamerica to ancient Egypt. Today, it's mostly used by Stevie Nicks fan club members and other Oregonians. A nice benefit is that the desperate-for-health can try it out while also building a fascinating and beautiful rock collection. Crystals are said to work by channeling certain energies of the universe directly into (or out of) your chakras—a series of "healing" points along your "spine." Though devotees pore over complex charts explaining which crystal placed upon which energy center clears up which malady, I recommend winging it. If you're feeling off, find a few different rocks—try looking outside, or at the bottom of an aquarium—and hold each on different places on your body until you feel better. Prettier rocks probably have more healing power.

TAP WATER THERAPY A 2008 Associated Press investigation found that our drinking water is loaded with medical run-off, including antibiotics, sedatives, anti-convulsants, mood stabilizers, and sex hormones. In other words, free drugs! Next time you're sick, skip the pharmacy and just elbow up to the kitchen sink. The way these drugs end up in our water is simple: most pharmaceuticals aren't fully absorbed by the body, so they pass into the sewer system, where water treatment facilities aren't equipped to remove them. Which means the AP is burying the real story: you're drinking recycled pee![34] That's something I might have found horrifying if I wasn't drinking a nice cold glass of Xanax-infused urine water.

MEDICINE

METH According to my most recent assumptions, over two dozen people in America currently

IF IT DOESN'T WORK, YOU HAVE A HEAD START ON THE BURIAL.

---

[33] Can't afford the whole rack? Just do a couple lines of Mrs. Dash, and you're good to go. Try new Fiesta Lime flavor!

[34] God, I hope it kills those brain-eating amoebas.

don't have healthcare. Luckily, the free market has stepped in and provided them with an alternative they can afford: Methamphetamines.

Keep in mind, this is a controlled substance—using it is illegal and dangerous. On the other hand, it's cheap, readily available, and after your teeth fall out, you'll save money on dentistry. Not only that, but when you buy homemade meth, you're no longer at the mercy of price-gouging Big Pharma. Just the mercy of Big Joe Bob from the barn out in the woods, and you can outrun him. At least the meth says you can.

Meth is made from ingredients found only in nature, and/or a local Pep Boys: like iodine, butane, Dran-O, battery acid, asthma medications, antifreeze, and soothing lavender. It's very easy to cook up a batch, especially if you're a bit of a Do-It-Yourselfer who enjoys burning down the garage.

Meth is so easy to make that people set up meth labs in their homes, in motel rooms, even in a car trunk. The car trunk-meth lab makes particular sense if you're already using your glove compartment to grow hydroponic pot. Open a drug rehab center in the back seat, and you've got yourself one hell of a vertically integrated Buick Skylark!

As for what ailments meth treats—what *doesn't* it treat?[35] It's a great cure for regular heartbeat, persistent night sleep, chronically appropriate emotions, acute responsibility, predictable libido, mealtime appetite syndrome and, of course, tooth-in-mouth disease. It's also a great pick-me-up for those days when you're just not in the mood to start a fight with a stranger or don't feel like scratching holes in your skin. Match that, 5-Hour Energy Drink!

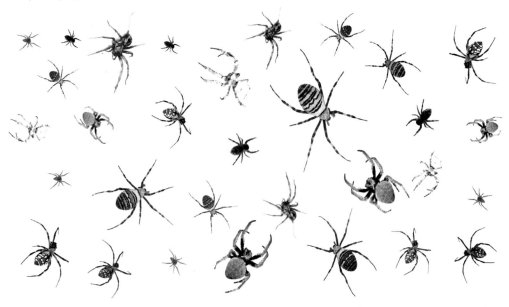

SPIDERS! SPIDERS! SPIDERS!

[35] Answer: Meth addiction

VETERINARY MEDICINE There's still one kind of doctor out there who went to a real school with tests and everything, but won't charge you an arm and a leg to fix your arm and leg: the vet. And he's good for more than just affordable vasectomies.

Of course, the vet may refuse to treat you on the technicality that you are not an animal—but technically you are! You shouldn't be discriminated against just because you were born without a cloaca.

Don't worry, there's a simple way to get around this detail and receive the medical attention you deserve. For less than the price of a regular doctor's co-pay, you can pick up a common housecat at the pet store. Take it to the vet and explain how the cat has been complaining of shooting pains in its legs ever since it lifted the TV cabinet last week, or how it has been feeling really stressed at work, or how it has trouble getting an erection. Fact is, pets receive many of the very same medications we do, often with the added benefit of de-worming agents. For more serious conditions requiring surgery, you may want to look into a high quality gorilla costume.

HEY, DOCTORS READING THIS!
DOES THIS MOLE LOOK SUSPICIOUS?

IT'S CHANGING SHAPE! LAST WEEK IT LOOKED LIKE JAVIER BARDEM AND THIS WEEK IT LOOKS LIKE ANTONIO BANDERAS. LEMME KNOW.

"I CAN HAZ DIABETEEZ?!"

 LAUGHTER, THE BEST MEDICINE (WHEN MEDICINE ISN'T AVAILABLE)

Anybody who has watched Dr. Gregory House (from the hit medical show *Greg*) has learned a thing or two. Firstly, it's never the first three diseases doctors think it is, which is why you should always start with a fourth opinion. And Dr. House's wacky life-endangering drug-addled antics remind us all: there is no better medicine than 20cc's of chuckles! With that in mind, I have written the following joke to help those of you who may be sick but don't have insurance:

A doctor says to his patient, "I've got good news and bad news. Which would you like first?" The patient says, "The bad news." The doctor says, "You've got a brain tumor, which is damaging your short-term memory retention." The patient thinks about this for a minute and says, "What's the good news?" The doctor says, "There isn't any, I was just hoping you'd forget I said that." The patient says "Forget you said what?" and they both have a good laugh, even though the patient isn't quite sure why he's laughing.

TURN YOUR HEAD AND SCOFF

While America has the greatest healthcare system in the world, there is inequality. One privileged group gets more access to treatment than anyone else. I think you know who I'm talking about: lab mice.

MUST BE NICE

These beady-eyed hypochondra-rats are somehow always first in line to get cancer cures new vaccines, erection treatments, anti-aging innovations and baldness breakthroughs. Sorry, I don't think our medical establishments' first priority should be ensuring mice aren't self-conscious about their receding furlines when they're ravaging our pantries. I say, man up, mice. Either get a transplant or shave your head like your predator, the New Orleans Swamp Python. (see photo) All our medical professionals are doing is breeding a super-race of immortal mice with lustrous heads of hair and erections that could chip tile.

And these super-rodents won't be brought down by disease, because scientists have also cured mouse Parkinson's, mouse paralysis,

and mouse AIDS, which just sends the message that they can stop using condoms. Scientists have even grown a mouse with an almost completely human liver, so now in addition to being able to out-maze us, they can drink us under the table.

Science, if you're going to pick an animal to give cutting-edge medical advances, at least go with dachshunds. I say we must spare no expense until we discover a way to make them longer. It'll be even more hilarious.

COULD BE FUNNIER

I've got an even better idea: you've got 50 million uninsured Americans out there, so why not cut out the middle-mouse and start doing these unregulated medical fishing expeditions on humans? It's perfect, after decades of not seeing a doctor, they'll come pre-riddled with a Whitman's Sampler of diseases. And what uninsured 25-year-old wouldn't want a giant ear on their back? Finally, another hole to toss some headphones in.

NEW ORLEANS SWAMP PYTHON

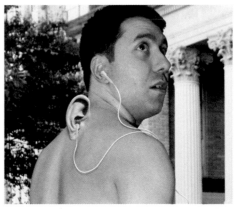

SPINAL SUBWOOFER

Of course, seeing a doctor is no guarantee that you're on the road to health. In fact, doctors are known to keep many things from their patients, which I covered in my bestseller:

OVER 30 MILLION COPIES PULPED

AS SEEN IN THIS BOOK!

Dr. Stephen T. Colbert, D.F.A.

WHAT YOUR "DOCTOR" ISN'T TELLING YOU™

UPDATED EDITION
INCLUDES WHAT NURSES ARE WHISPERING BEHIND YOUR BACK™

WHAT YOUR "DOCTOR" ISN'T TELLING YOU™

Doctors like to throw around a lot of mumbo jumbo you can't understand without a medical degree. They do this for one reason only: to make themselves feel better for wasting their 20s studying corpses while the rest of us were enjoying our lives.

A classic example is your cholesterol number. To the layperson, it's meaningless. But a simple process can uncover the Secrets They Don't Want You To Know About.™

> **TAKE THIS SIMPLE TEST TO DETERMINE WHETHER YOU REALLY NEED TO WORRY ABOUT YOUR CHOLESTEROL LEVEL.**

❶ Take the meaningless total cholesterol level your doctor gave you and write it down as a 3-digit number. (If it's 89, write 089. If it's over 1000, you are already dead.) If the first and last digits of your cholesterol are the same, add 1.

❷ Reverse the digits of this number, to get your lucky number. Write it down.

❸ Subtract the smaller number from the larger one, and write down the result. This is your Cholesterol Difference Quotient, which is a number *Your Doctor Is Withholding*.™

❹ Reverse the digits of your CDQ to get your Inverse CDQ, *A Powerful Number Your Doctors are Keeping to Themselves*.™

❺ Add your CDQ to your Inverse CDQ to calculate your Cholesterol Index Level, a number *Your Doctor Doesn't Want You to Know*.™

❻ Add all of the digits of your CIL together. For example, if it is 1234, you would add 1+2+3+4=10. This number is your Essential Cholesterol, which is a *Secret Your Doctor Isn't Telling You*.™

❼ What your doctor *really* doesn't want you to know is that you are completely healthy, and have nothing to worry about as long as your Essential Cholesterol isn't 18. If your EC is 18, you could drop dead at any moment. I urge you to run, don't walk to your computer to order Dr. Stephen T. Colbert, D.F.A.'s Life-Extending Fish Oil Cholesterol-Blasting Omega-3 Multivitamin Artery Auger, available from Prescott Pharmaceuticals and participating Jiffy Lubes. Only **$49.99** for a 12-week supply. Call now! Your life is at risk—not that your doctor would ever tell you that.

WALL STREET

fig 22.3-D. **STEPHEN COLBERT**

CHAPTER FOUR

WALL STREET

"MONEY IS THE ROOT OF ALL EVIL."

*—Don't know who said it, but I'm
guessing he never drove an Audi S5*

Clang! Clang! Clang! Clang! Clang! Clang! Clang!
Clang! Clang! Clang! Clang! Clang! Clang! Clang!
Clang! Clang! Clang! Clang! Clang! Clang! Clang!
Clang! Clang! Clang! Clang! Clang! Clang! Clang!
Clang! Clang! Clang! Clang! Clang! Clang! Clang!
Clang! Clang! Clang! Clang! Clang![1]

That's the sound of Wall Street's opening bell.
And it's the sound of the opening of this chapter.[2]

When that bell clangs at 9:30, it signals the start of the Greatest Drama on Earth.
The setting: America. The hero: cash. Every dollar, yen, euro, dinar, peso, and
Africa money[3] in the world embarks on a lightning-fast pilgrimage to downtown
Manhattan, where it leaps from day-trader to kindly plutocrat to greedy retiree
to the genetically enhanced babies chained in the laboratories of the E*Trade
marketing department, until the closing bell rings, and it finally comes to rest,
tucked into the marsupial G-strings of the lovely ladies of The New York Dolls
Club. What a rush.[4]

---

[1] Clang!

[2] Note to publisher: Insert a hinge-activated sound chip to play a recording of the Wall Street bell
when this page is turned to by the reader. THIS IS IMPORTANT TO ME. Otherwise, those 40 "Clangs!"
I put up there are a waste of our nation's precious ink reserves. I AM TRUSTING YOU!

[3] "Africash?" It should be.

[4] A "Rush" will cost you $100 at New York Dolls.

GOLDMAN SACHS CEO LLOYD BLANKFEIN RINGS THE OPENING BELL

But there's another group of heroes: the hardworking men and women of Wall Street's hedge buildings, investment exchangeries, and stock banks—regular folks who rise at the crack of dawn and hit the NYSE floor to do a job no one else can: posing for photos of dejected brokers for articles about the latest bubble collapse.

Computers do most of the actual trading.[5] And thank goodness they do. Because computers allow us to make tens of thousands of trades per second—precious seconds we otherwise would have wasted wondering if we'd really meant to push "enter" instead of "delete." And more important, those computers securely encrypt every transaction, protecting both buyer and seller from the risk of accountability. Imagine if the engineers who designed that software had wasted their careers at NASA![6]

Wall Street is the engine of the American economy. It's the greatest American institution

WAIT, DID I SAY "MILLION" OR "BILLION?"

[5] And if the police ask, most of the cocaine.
[6] Everyone wants to be as *smart* as a rocket scientist. But as *poor* as one? No, thanks.

ever given to us by the Dutch. Originally called "de Waal Straat," because the Dutch couldn't be bothered with *spelling*—they were busy recovering from the collapse of the world's first speculative bubble: Tulip Mania!

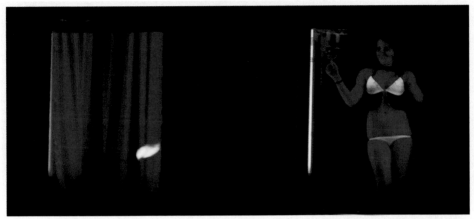

SADLY, MANY DUTCH INVESTORS LOST THEIR SHIRTS IN THE TULIP CRASH

The Dutch also built the famous wall to keep out hostile Indians, the original 99 Percent, because just like the Occupy protesters, they had drum circles, camped out in tents, and were eventually evicted by armed white people.

Now, I hear their criticism. Mainly because I'm dictating this to Siri on a luxurious hotel balcony overlooking an Occupy Protest.[7] Excuse me a moment while I relate to the Common Man.

Hello, down there! Crumbs to the Man and Up with Hey-Hey-Ho-Ho!

They love me. But, of course, we don't see eye to eye on everything.[8] For instance, those folks don't understand why Wall Street Job Creators take home million-dollar bonuses while those who work in unskilled sectors, like child-

FACT

Founding Father Alexander Hamilton is buried in Wall Street's Trinity Church graveyard. Legend has it that if you leave a ten-dollar bill on his gravestone on the anniversary of his death, when you return the next day... the money will be gone!

---

[7] Note to Ed.: If the Occupy Movement has been neutralized at the time of publication, replace with "a peaceful and prosperous shanty cluster."

[8] Thanks to my monocle.

teaching, barely earn enough to afford their treasured "cheez" snacks. Well, the reason is obvious. Wall Street guys get the most money because *they work right next to all the money.* Every dollar in the world flows right through their offices so, naturally, they get first dibs on dipping their ladles in the stream. It's only fair. Meanwhile, if you're sitting on your keister way out in a St. Louis public school, you can't be surprised if, by the time the money flow reaches you, it's slowed to a dribble. Or that someone upstream pooped in it.

If the Occupy Wall Street had one message, it was, **"MY EYES! IT'S BURNING MY EYES!"** But the second message was, "We are the 99%."[9] Well I'm sorry, folks, but that's...

CLASS WARFARE!

Class warfare is tearing this country apart. Oh, the 99 percenters love to yell, *"Hey man, I heard that America's income disparity is worse than the Ivory Coast's!"* First, have you been to the Ivory Coast? They have amazing beaches! Just don't leave the resort, or the locals will machete your clavicle. They're just jealous. They want to punish the wealthy for their success. Well, I earned my money fair and square, and I am proud of every

CAN I GET YOU A MARGARITA? OR IF I SEE YOU IN TOWN LATER, ALL OF YOUR CASH AND HIGH RESALE ORGANS?

nickel. If you don't like the fact that I have more wealth than the combined resources of every generation of your family that will ever exist, sue me.

ASK FOR "THE SEC VIOLATION." THE SAFE WORD IS "BERNANKE."

We'll see who can afford the better lawyer. Besides, Wall Street bankers have already been punished for their success. Her name is Madame Carlotta, and she is extremely discreet.

According to a Pew Research poll, two-thirds of Americans think the rich and poor are in conflict. And that number would have been even higher but a lot of billionaires can't get decent cell reception in their panic rooms.

What kind of society punishes hard working job creators and rewards non-contributing losers? Money is the lifeblood of our economy. Wall Streeters are the heart—they do all the work. So, they should get to keep

---

[9] Third was "Can you watch my bongos while I go crap behind Chipotle?"

all the blood. Everyone knows that the healthiest body is the one where all the blood has pooled in the heart (See my diagram!). The heart earned that blood, and why should it have to share it with the lazy feet, hands, brain, and those do-nothing kidneys, who just piss it away all the time? Not to mention that slacker appendix, which hasn't held down a real job since the Paleolithic.

SELF-PORTRAITS IN COURAGE:
INVESTMENT BANKER

I bet you didn't know that Wall Streeters earn their massive bonuses with 18-hour stress-filled days, where the smallest mistake can mean a multibillion-dollar loss, and the banker is personally on the hook for as much as none of it.

DIAGRAM:
A HUMAN BODY SWOLLEN
WITH HEALTH!

For the real story on a banker's day, we turn to my friend and polo teammate, Brenton Kunnelthorpe IV.

He agreed to participate on the condition that his boat remains anonymous.[10]

BRENTON. PHOTO TAKEN
IMMEDIATELY AFTER
FIRING SOMEONE

DIARY
STARTS ON NEXT PAGE

---

[10] For the record, it's called *The Sea Douche*.

5:30 AM WAKE UP, HAVE COFFEE, THEN HAVE MUFFIN. PAY HER.

6:00 AM I GET OUT OF BED AND PUT ON MY SLIPPERS, MADE FROM THE FORCED CROSS-BREEDING OF A MINK AND AN UGG.

6:10 AM THE BREAKFAST OF CHAMPIONS: EGGS COOKED BY 1996 GOLD-MEDALIST MICHAEL JOHNSON. THE FOOD'S TERRIBLE, BUT TO BE HONEST I'M PAYING FOR THE LOOK ON HIS FACE WHEN I REMIND HIM TO PUT ON HIS CHEF'S HAT.

6:42 AM I CHECK MY BLACKBERRY AND DELETE EVERYTHING FROM SPAMMERS, MARKET REGULATORS, OR FAMILY MEMBERS.
THEN I FIRE OFF AN EMAIL APPROVING THE DISMANTLING OF A FAMILY-OWNED TOY FACTORY, HITTING SEND WHILE POINTING A FINGER GUN AT THE SCREEN.

7:00 AM LIMO ARRIVES TO TAKE ME TO WORK. I PUNCH MY DRIVER IN THE FACE, THEN WRITE HIM A CHECK FOR $20,000.

7:45 AM ARRIVE AT THE OFFICE FEELING LIKE A MILLION BUCKS. WHICH, BY THE STANDARDS OF MY PROFESSION, PUTS ME IN A TERRIBLE MOOD.

8:30 AM REVIEW THE PRESENTATIONS AND PITCHBOOKS THAT JUNIOR ANALYSTS STAYED UP ALL NIGHT WRITING IN SLEEP-DEPRIVED FUGUE STATES. I KNOW THEY WATCH ME THROUGH MY OFFICE WINDOWS, SO I KEEP THEM ON THEIR TOES BY SETTING ONE DOCUMENT ON FIRE.

9:10 AM I SIGN TEN PIECES OF PAPER, LOOK BACK OVER THE SECOND PIECE OF PAPER LIKE I'VE SEEN SOMETHING, RUN MY FINGER OVER IT WITH A CAUTIOUS LOOK ON MY FACE, TOUCH MY CHIN, ONCE, TWICE, THEN STACK THE PAPERS BACK UP AND NOD APPROVINGLY. I CAN MAKE THIS PROCESS TAKE AS LITTLE AS 30 SECONDS OR AS LONG AS TWO AND A HALF HOURS.

11:40 AM I TELL MY ASSISTANT I'M GOING TO THE GYM. ON THE WAY, I WALK INTO A FIRST-YEAR ANALYST'S OFFICE AND DEMAND HE COMPUTE THE AGGREGATE ROE YIELDS OF EVERY SALMON FARM IN SCOTLAND. I WAIT UNTIL HIS FACE REACHES ITS PEAK MOMENT OF EXHAUSTED FRUSTRATION BEFORE DEPLOYING THE LINE, "HEY, SOMETIMES YOU'VE GOT TO SWIM UPSTREAM." THEN I MAKE HIM HIGH-FIVE ME.

11:50 AM GYM. MY TRAINER, A HALF-NAKED THAI FEMALE KICKBOXING CHAMPION, STRAPS ELECTRODES ONTO MY PECS AND CRANKS THE DIAL TO "RIP CITY," AND I WATCH WHILE SHE MAKES SHORT WORK OF BROCK LESNAR.

1:00 PM LUNCH. LIKE TO KEEP IT CLASSY. I BUY A P'ZONE, GO TO PER SE, AND MAKE THE CHEF SERVE IT TO ME AS A PER'ZONE.

CHEF TEARS

2:45 PM I CHECK MY BLACKBERRY AGAIN. I'D CALL IT A COMPULSIVE BEHAVIOR, BUT THAT WOULD BE AN INSULT TO MY COKE ADDICTION.

PER ZONE STAIN

3:00 PM BACK TO THE OFFICE, GOT A PRETTY GOOD GIN BUZZ GOING. MIGHT BUY A PHARMACEUTICAL COMPANY, WHICH IS FINANCE LINGO FOR SNORTING TWO ADDERALL AND THEN BUYING A PHARMACEUTICAL COMPANY.

♡ *Mr.* ♡
Lloyd ♡
Kunnellthorpe

3:10 PM CONFERENCE CALL WITH SEC REGULATORS. GREAT TIME TO NAP OR CATCH UP ON MY COMPUTER PORN.

4:00 PM STEP OUT FOR COFFEE FROM A CAFÉ THAT REQUIRES A PASSWORD TO GET IN, BECAUSE THEY HAVE ONE OF THOSE ASIAN COFFEE-POOPING CATS CHAINED UP IN BACK.

4:15 PM TIME FOR A LITTLE BUSINESS GOLF WITH THE IRANIANS.

4:25 PM DRILL A SEVEN-FOOT PUTT, FLEX MY BICEPS, AND SCREAM "THAT'S FOR THE HOSTAGE CRISIS, MOTHERFUCKERS!"

6:15 PM DESTROY THE ECONOMY OF GREECE

8:00 PM DINNER AT A PLACE WHERE A DIVER JUMPS INTO A CENTRAL WATER TANK AND KNIFES THE MERMAID YOU'VE CHOSEN.

11:00 PM I SWING BACK BY THE OFFICE IN TIME TO TELL THE SALMON ANALYST—ONE FOOT OUT THE DOOR AT THIS POINT—THAT HE'D BETTER GO AHEAD AND CROSS-REFERENCE HIS ROE NUMBERS WITH CAVIAR PROJECTIONS FROM RUSSIAN BLACK MARKET STURGEON CONGLOMERATES. I THINK. I'M PRETTY HAMMERED AT THIS POINT.

12:00 AM MIDNIGHT MUFFIN

12:30 AM LONDON MARKETS OPEN IN HALF AN HOUR, SO I PREPARE BY DOING A LINE OF BLOW OFF THE COVER OF THE SECRET EIGHTH HARRY POTTER BOOK. JACKED ENOUGH TO FIGHT DUMBLEDORE.

1:01 AM LONDON MARKETS OPEN. I AM IMMEDIATELY RUINED, AND JUMP OUT MY WINDOW, BUT I AM SAVED BY LANDING ON THE SALMON ROE ANALYST.

1:30 AM CONTEMPLATE WHETHER WHAT I DO SERVES SOCIETY IN ANY WAY.

1:31 AM ASLEEP.

Mr.
Brenoyd
Kunnelfein?

NOTES:
_____
_____
_____
_____

July 2013						
S	M	T	W	T	F	S
	1	2	3	4	5	6
7	8	9	10	11	12	13
14	15	16	17	18	19	20
21	22	23	24	25	26	27
28	29	30	31			

August 2013						
S	M	T	W	T	F	S
				1	2	3
4	5	6	7	8	9	10
11	12	13	14	15	16	17
18	19	20	21	22	23	24
25	26	27	28	29	30	31

September 2013						
S	M	T	W	T	F	S
1	2	3	4	5	6	7
8	9	10	11	12	13	14
15	16	17	18	19	20	21
22	23	24	25	26	27	28
29	30					

THE FINANCIAL WHOOPSIE DAISY:

AKA THE SINGLE GREATEST GLOBAL FINANCIAL DISASTER SINCE THE GREAT DEPRESSION

Now, I'm going to ask you to do something I normally don't believe in: **Take a Step Back**. Reason I don't normally believe in it? It exposes the tender flesh of the inner thigh to a *tae kwon do* chop. But it's important to do here. Because when you look at the **Big Picture of Wall Street**—the undisputed hub of global finance, where the brightest minds gather to buy and sell everything that exists—one thing becomes clear: Wall Street bears no responsibility for the worldwide economic collapse.[11]

What you *do* see is industrious, modest men and women who are ripe for exploitation by the poor. As CNBC Street Squawker Rick Santelli famously said from the heart of Real America,[13] real Americans got duped into bailing out irresponsible borrowers who took out loans to pay for luxuries they couldn't afford, like shelter.

Yes, the sad truth is, Wall Streeters are easy marks for fly-by-night con artists who hide out below the poverty line.

Take the infamous Wall Street "meltdown" of 2008. Here's how the scam worked: the poor set up a roadside shop labeled "The American Dream." Then they lured Wall Street rubes into handing over low interest-rate mortgages, no questions asked, and duped those same bankers into repackaging those mortgages into insanely overvalued tradable securities *(See page 105)*. Oldest trick in the book. When the whole thing crumbled, taking the global economy with it

RICK SANTELLI, HOME AFFORDER

(and make no mistake: poor people **hate** the global economy), the poor laughed all the way to the bank, which as it happened, their taxes now paid to operate. Game, Set, Match!

---

[11] *Tae kwon do* chop![12]

[12] (I warned you!)

[13] AKA the floor of the Chicago Mercantile Exchange.

The real goal of the poor was to drag unsuspecting Wall Street execs down to their level. And after the collapse, they did it by forcing Wall Street to swallow the largest welfare check in U.S. history: $7 trillion in government cheese. Total humiliation. "Now we're all on Uncle Sam's dole, mother(cursing)s!" the poor all yell in delight in the mural I had commissioned for my greatroom wall.

YOU'VE WON THIS ROUND, POOR...

Of course, unlike the poor, Wall Streeters accepted their welfare with humility. That's why you never hear them mention it these days.

"But Stephen," you're wondering, "I thought these guys were savvy operators. How did they get tricked? Aren't they the ones who know how our financial system really works?"

"Plus," you go on, "you know all the top Wall Street people. What's *their* explanation for what happened?" First of all, this is my book. I do the talking. I know those big shots. And I am happy to share what I've learned from the top minds on Wall Street: **Nobody** knows how Wall Street works.

BEATS ME!

That's **why** it works. Same reason the Ancient Israelites quaked before their wrathful God. Like Yahweh, the ways of the Dow are impenetrable to man's mind. When we pay obeisance to It, It rewards us with prosperity. When we turn our hearts from It in the form of regulation, Its fury is infinite. To appease It we must not question It. To show our fealty, something must be sacrificed. Your job, for instance.[14]

So heed my words, gentle reader.[15] To those who say Wall Street incompetence was responsible for the collapse of our economy, consider this: after the crisis, *finance is the one industry in America that continued to thrive while the rest of the economy sank into oblivion.* I'd say that proves Wall Street knows exactly what it's doing.[16]

RISE OF THE MACHINES:
LACK-OF-HUMAN-JUDGEMENT DAY

One reason Wall Street manages to keep making money, even as your neighborhood devolves into a Michael Moore documentary, is that they've removed virtually all human compassion from the trading process by letting computers make all the decisions.[17]

"YOUR DESPAIR WON THE PALME D'OR!"

The computer age has brought incredible leaps forward in the technology that makes Wall Street run. Advances like artificial intelligence, pattern recognition, logic trees, and virtual pets have all made their way to the trading desks, revolutionizing our markets in ways that we are only beginning to pat ourselves on the back for.

YOUR PENSION
FUND MANAGER.
DONT FORGET
TO FEED HIM!

Those in the Windows™ generation are familiar with Clippy, the animated paperclip, who would appear onscreen and cheerily ask, for instance, "It looks like you're trying to write a résumé. Can I help you?" Now, imagine if the same charming office supply appeared and instead asked:

---

[14] Oh, Ye of little capital.

[15] You too, rough guy.

[16] And therefore, is blameless for what it knew it did.

[17] 1U: Make money, 20. GOTO 10

It looks like you're trying to capitalize on a temporary unexplained dip in the price of a particular commodity. Can I help you by momentarily selling a portfolio of stocks that might be affected by those commodity prices until they adjust themselves, at which time I'll trade again in tandem with other counter-trades without human input at incredibly high speeds?

Now, imagine that instead of a person saying "What?" Clippy is instantly answered by another computer, with its own hyper-intelligent Clippy, and that thousands of these transactions are made every microsecond, accounting for more than two-thirds of trading volume on the New York Stock Exchange. The official name is algorithmic trading, but I like to think of it as the Transformers playing Texas Hold 'Em!

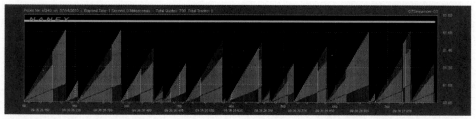

SINGLE STOCK BEING COMPUTER-TRADED HUNDREDS OF TIMES OVER 6/10ᵀᴴ OF A SECOND. ALSO KIND OF LOOKS LIKE A REGATTA. SEE YOU AT THE CAPE!

There have been some bumps on the road to Wall Street's digital-re-pavement. On May 6, 2010, the markets were spooked by the so-called "Flash Crash," when the Dow Jones lost 1,000 points in just minutes, only to rebound less than a half-hour later. It was a terrifying plunge, with the market taking a 9 percent hit in less time than it takes to change the pants you just soiled. Now, because so much of the trading was automated, it was difficult to determine what triggered the mass sell-off. So the good news is we don't know what happened, therefore it will never happen again.

THE DOW JONES: AMERICA'S EKG

Folks, there are plenty of ways to assess the health of the market. Are sales of durable goods down? Are new housing starts sluggish? What color is Jim Cramer's face?

But far and away, the best and most trusted economic indicator is the **DOW JONES INDUSTRIAL AVERAGE.** As a market expert, I know that the Dow takes the pulse of the market by, I wanna say, counting Dows? And then dividing that by...Joneses? It's complicated.

WHEN HIS HEAD STARTS BLENDING INTO THE SET, SELL!

All you need to know is that if the Dow closes up, things are good.

"MY GIRLFRIEND LEFT ME FOR A PORKPIE!"

If it closes down, it might be time to make a mental list of which daughter you'd be willing to sell.[18]

So we don't really know why the Dow does what it Dows, we just know it's incredibly sensitive and prone to volatility. A world event like the Euro Crisis, or even subtle changes in consumer confidence, can send it surging or plummeting. It's sort of like your manic cousin Gabe, who can be super fun at family events, but can also be set off at the drop of a hat. Because, why'd you drop that hat?! You know **FULL WELL** Gabe has a thing about hats!

---

[18] The mouthy one.

EVENTS THAT CAUSED SWINGS IN THE DOW

1900–2012

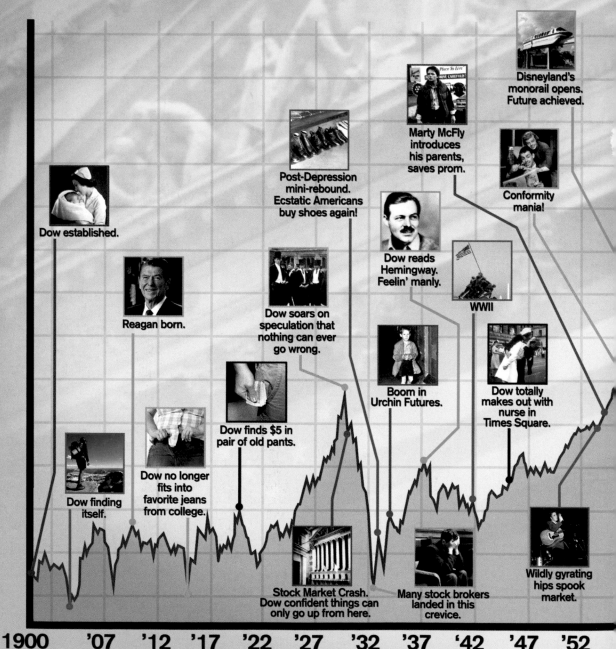

Disneyland's monorail opens. Future achieved.

Marty McFly introduces his parents, saves prom.

Conformity mania!

Post-Depression mini-rebound. Ecstatic Americans buy shoes again!

Dow reads Hemingway. Feelin' manly.

Dow established.

WWII

Reagan born.

Dow soars on speculation that nothing can ever go wrong.

Boom in Urchin Futures.

Dow totally makes out with nurse in Times Square.

Dow finds $5 in pair of old pants.

Dow no longer fits into favorite jeans from college.

Dow finding itself.

Stock Market Crash. Dow confident things can only go up from here.

Many stock brokers landed in this crevice.

Wildly gyrating hips spook market.

| 1900 | '07 | '12 | '17 | '22 | '27 | '32 | '37 | '42 | '47 | '52 |

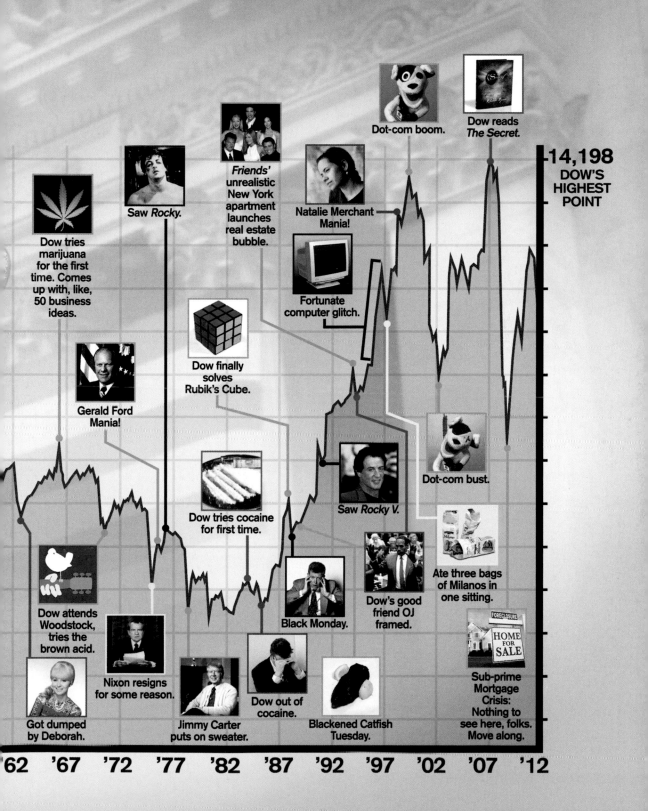

Dow tries marijuana for the first time. Comes up with, like, 50 business ideas.

Saw *Rocky*.

Friends' unrealistic New York apartment launches real estate bubble.

Natalie Merchant Mania!

Dot-com boom.

Dow reads *The Secret.*

14,198
DOW'S HIGHEST POINT

Gerald Ford Mania!

Dow finally solves Rubik's Cube.

Fortunate computer glitch.

Dow tries cocaine for first time.

Saw *Rocky V.*

Dot-com bust.

Dow attends Woodstock, tries the brown acid.

Got dumped by Deborah.

Nixon resigns for some reason.

Jimmy Carter puts on sweater.

Dow out of cocaine.

Black Monday.

Blackened Catfish Tuesday.

Dow's good friend OJ framed.

Ate three bags of Milanos in one sitting.

Sub-prime Mortgage Crisis: Nothing to see here, folks. Move along.

'62 '67 '72 '77 '82 '87 '92 '97 '02 '07 '12

WORKING ON THE EXCHANGE FLOOR:
~~ A HAND-Y GUIDE TO HAND SIGNALS ~~

As I mentioned before, today 60% of Wall Street trades are made via superfast computers[19] which cannot and should not be held responsible for any wrongdoing. But there are still a few exchanges that rely on something called "humans" (See Figure A). These markets operate by an old system known as Open Outcry, where traders relay their orders in the trading pit via a series of shouts and hand signals. It's a throwback to a simpler time, when world-shattering financial crises were made by hand! Below are some examples of the hand signals still in use.

FIGURE A:
A HUMAN PERSON

"BUY."

"SELL."

"STOP THE ORDER."

"BUY HOG FUTURES."

---

[19] At least that's the statistic my computer gave me.

"HELP! I AM CHOKING!"

"INVEST IN TURTLENECKS."

"ASIAN MARKETS ARE OPEN!"

"WHAT? I'M NOT A RACIST."

"THERE'S A DOG LOOSE ON
THE TRADING FLOOR."

"I HAVE ROYALLY SCREWED MY
INVESTORS IN THE POOPER."

"EVERYTHING IS JUST FINE. JUST PLEASE,
FOR THE LOVE OF GOD, KEEP INVESTING!"

"I'VE BEEN CAUGHT INSIDER-TRADING.
IF YOU NEED ME, I'LL BE IN DISGUISE
IN BUENOS AIRES UNDER THE NAME
SEÑOR DOMINGO."

HEDGE FUNDS

Since Wall Street represents everything that's best about America, we can imagine it as another great institution: a private country club that Wall Street executives belong to. That's called a metaphor. And those of us who belong to these exclusive clubs love metaphors—*as if we were cats and the metaphors were crystal goblets of high-class cat food.* Bam! Membership renewed. See, just like a metaphorical country club full of smart guys using metaphors, Wall Street attracts only the best kind of people. At the club, it doesn't matter where you grew up or what religion you practice (now that the plaintiffs have signed the non-disclosure agreement). All that matters is that you share the values of your fellow members and that you love golf, which in this metaphor, is investing. And as anyone at my club will tell you, investing is a great metaphor for golf.

But even though all members of the club are equal, there are certain members who are much better than everyone else. They are so skilled at golf—investing—that they don't have to play by the rules.

These folks gather in small, anonymous groups that are allowed to tee off from the green, hide land mines in the sand traps, and use other exotic and risky strategies, like descending into the spirit world to capture and subjugate Bagger Vance.

FINANCIAL ADVISOR/
METAPHOR FOR
WHITE GUILT

On Wall Street, these groups are known as **Hedge Funds**, and if you want to join them, you've got to pay big. The minimum investment required for the average Hedge Fund is $1 million.

But it's worth every penny. Because when you're part of a Hedge Fund, you benefit from the finest, most opaque investment strategies in the world. See, Hedge Funds are where the brightest minds on Wall Street apply the precise mathematical formula they've devised to outperform the market every time:

$$\text{BIGGEST CASH PILE} + \text{SMARTEST PEOPLE} - \text{CAPACITY FOR EMPATHY} = \text{MAD DOLLA\$!}$$

How do I know so much? Fine, you got me. I'm in a Hedge Fund. It's not easy to sneak my enormous wealth past a sharp customer like you. And since we've come this far, I might as well lead you into the inner sanctum and expose my tender secrets, exactly as I do at our annual Hedge Fund Conclave's Welcome Orgy. Here's how it works: me and a couple of close friends—Donald Rumsfeld, Star Jones, Saudi Intelligence Director Prince Muqrin bin Abdul-Aziz, Sting, and Louis C.K.—have invested significant sums with a genius hedge fund manager whose name I cannot divulge, mainly because I do not know it. Standard Hedge Fund agreement. But I do know that his work at SkyBrigand LLC is as superb as it is impenetrable. Using his super-mind, he combs the market for companies, industries, nations, or continents that are about to lose value, and then engages in a sophisticated maneuver known as "**short selling**," or "**shorting**," for short. I'll try my best to explain it, but you'll have to wade through some extremely esoteric and complicated financial jargon. He uses *money*[20] to place a *bet*[21] that something's *price*[22] will go *down*.[23] I'll wait while you collect your brains from the wall they were just blown onto.

Short selling allows Hedge Funds to rack up huge gains even while the rest of the economy collapses around them, thus insulating us super-rich from the cataclysmic market swings that someone always seems to be causing. I'm guessing illegal immigrants.

And you can trust the Hedge Fund guys. Because when you invest with them, you're rolling with the best of the best, because all of the most intelligent people are putting all of the most intelligent people into Hedge Funds. These "quants"—short for "quants who run Hedge Funds"—often have advanced university degrees in mathematics and physics, but decided to leave the Ivory Tower for something much more rewarding: living in a tower made of ivory. And they always get it right. The rewards: huge. The size of the hugeness: large. And all Hedge Fund managers ask in return for this noble

DON'T PRETEND YOU
DON'T KNOW ABOUT
HEDGES, PEDRO!

service is that they become billionaires. And pay no more than 15% in taxes. And that their investors never call them on the phone, address them by name, or engage in direct eye contact. And that they tell you when you can have your goddamn investment back. But you'll never regret it, because you know the old saying at the club: Let's play golf (money)!

---

[20] What Time is.

[21] A Gamble.

[22] The cost of a thing.

[23] Not up.

KYLE SCOTT
Master Day Trader

You. Stop reading. You can't handle this. May as well hike up your diaper, wipe your tears with your bib and move on to the next section.

Still reading? Good. That was a test. You've got the balls to disobey an order like that. You might be cut out for the high-paced, fast-stakes world of day trading. Now, stop reading and move on to the next section.

Still reading? That was another test. And this time you failed. You got a little too cocky, kid. You can't let your emotions get the best of you when you're a day trader. 80% of day traders don't make money. They're the sheep, getting sheared by the 20% of us who are the sharks. We sharks gobble up those sheep when they get too close to the ocean, just like in nature.

I'm a master day trader. I spend all day in front of my screens, getting the pure rush of adrenaline that comes from knowing you're putting everything you own on which way a squiggly line is going to squiggle. I'm trading right now.

Oh, crap... hold on a second. I think I see a stock about to surge. Buy buy buy buy! Yes. Now, hold it... hold it, Kyle.... think about baseball... just a few seconds more... okay... and... sell sell sell sell! Yes!

I just made a sweet 18 bucks. Minus the 8 dollar trading fee on both the buy and the sell, but still: Two bucks, and I've only been at it for three hours today.

Tyler, what are you doing in Daddy's work room? No, it's Aunt Helen's room when Aunt Helen is visiting! The rest of the time it's Daddy's work room! Let Daddy work. Go find Mommy.

The secret is to watch the market and when you see movement go in for the kill, making short-term purchases that get liquidated by the end of the day. We wait for a stock to swing one way or another, then the party starts. And just like any swinger's party, it's exciting, dangerous, and you end up satisfied, crying, or both. The key is to keep your eye on the prize and stay focu—Shit shit shit shit sell sell SELL SELL SELL SELL.... hahahaHAA! Try to duck below 30 on me, will you, PRZ? Nice try. See? Lightning-fast reflexes, and now I didn't lose a dime more than everything I put in. That's how I roll, bro. I'm everywhere.

Day Trading is a skill that comes from the gut. No time for prospectuses or business plans. I'm flyin' bareback. Thinking about investing in a company? Just check their website: Does the "Contact Us" page have a hot chick wearing a headset? Then buy, buy, buy!

HER MOUTH SAYS "HELLO" BUT HER EYES SAY "GOOD BUY."

If I had to describe Day Trading in one word, it would be: totally kickass. If you say that's more than one word, well, you're not saying it the fast way I am. I've taken four Red Bulls, mixed them with a 5-Hour Energy Drink and a glass of hand-squeezed ginseng, put it in a food dehydrator, and snorted the dust. So "totally kickass" isn't just one word, it's one syllable.

Here's the secret: you don't have to know anything about investments. Day trading isn't about what stock is rising or falling, or even why. You just see that wave and you ride it. If there were some metaphor for riding waves, I'd use it. I guess it's like kayaking on a wave.

Shit! Squiggling! There's squiggling! How did I miss that?! God damn it, Tyler! Nope, he's not here. God damn it, person reading this! Okay. Okay, get it back. Back on the bitch! That's trader lingo for "back on the horse." Here we go. GXRC is dipping low. Oh, I'm on it. Come to Papa. $26.50. $26.25. $25.75. And LUNGE! Now we wait for the rebound.

If you walked into my trading room, you would feel the electricity in the air. Literally. Got 15 monitors. There's so much radiation flying around, I gotta wrap my balls in foil. I'm watching every major index, the latest data from Bloomberg. Over here I'm playing *Call of Duty*. And of course, Fox Business and CNBC—with the latest financial news, like this story about the CFO of GXRC getting indicted for securities fraud fuck fuck fuck sell sell SELL SELL SELL! Motherf—it's OK. It's OK. All part of the game. Gotta lose money to make money. The more you lose the more you make. Oh, god...

Time to go into Daddy's special stash of "Pixy Stix." Kick it into overdrive.

Tyler, get in here! Tyler? Buddy? Do you still have that birthday money Aunt Helen sent you?

<u>OOPS!</u>

As I have previously proven, America's Capitalist System is a faultless, perfect prosperity machine that can do no wrong. But there was a time in recent history when, to the uneducated observer, it went a little catawampus.[24] In September of 2008, just negative four months into Barack Obama's presidency, the markets collapsed.

You see, during the real estate boom, banks were forced by Big Government and their buddies, the poor, to issue subprime home mortgages. So, to make the best of an insanely profitable situation, the banks bundled these risky mortgages and some safer loans together, then resold them as financial instruments called Collateralized Debt Obligations, or CDOs.

These CDOs were divided into various layers of risk, or tranches, with the riskiest, but highest yielding, layers made up of just the subprime mortgages. Then the banks discovered a magic secret: they could bundle nothing but these riskiest loans and suddenly they would become safe loans. The secret to how this worked is that it did not work. But until it didn't, banks made a lot of money, and people got homes. It was so great that all the banks started selling these bundled CDOs to each other, then re-bundled the bundles to resell them to other re-bundlers.

Then, the unthinkable happened. Someone (I believe Bill Farber of Eugene, Oregon—we're checking) missed a mortgage payment, and $17 trillion instantly evaporated from the world economy. Investors started to suspect that some of those bundled CDOs contained toxic debt.[25] But at that point, nobody knew which CDOs had it, who owed that debt, how much they owed, what was safe, or what the deal was with that weird smoke monster on *Lost*.[26]

Confused? Well, just think of Wall Street as a giant church bake sale, only with less backstabbing. And think of Collateralized Debt Obligations as the brownie table. All sorts of folks have brought brownies to sell, mostly to each other.

WALL STREET

But Mrs. Havermeyer has a secret recipe. When she makes brownies, she puts a

---

[24] Actual word, as used in the sentence, "I confused my readers with the word *catawampus*."

[25] "Toxic" is a financial term meaning "without value or merit," named after the Britney Spears song of the same name and quality.

[26] Remember: it was 2008.

little bit of shit in her batter. Not a lot, just a little. That lets her turn a bigger profit on her brownies because baking with shit saves her money on more expensive ingredients, like things that don't come out of your anus.

All the other bakers see how much profit Mrs. Havermeyer is making, so they buy her shit batter and mix it with their own, and, naturally, put shit in their own batter to sell to each other. And everything goes fine, until Reverend Smithson bites into a brownie and says, **"Oh my God! This is shit!"**

At this point, no one can remember which brownies don't have shit in them, and boom: suddenly, nobody's buying brownies, and the bake sale collapses.[27]

SHIT-EATING GRIN

MRS. HAVERMEYER'S BROWNIES

INGREDIENTS:

2	CUPS WHITE SUGAR
1	TEASPOON VANILLA EXTRACT
1	CUP BUTTER
½	TEASPOON BAKING SODA
1½	CUPS COCOA POWDER
½	TEASPOON SALT
4	EGGS
1½	CUPS ALL-PURPOSE FLOUR
1-20	POUNDS HUMAN FECES (MAY CONTAIN NUTS)

DIRECTIONS:

1. PREHEAT OVEN TO 350°
2. MIX ALL INGREDIENTS IN LARGE BOWL
3. POOP IN BOWL
4. BAKE FOR 30 MINUTES
5. SELL (DO NOT MENTION POOP)

---

[27] Mrs. Havermeyer is given a $5,000,000 bonus to keep her talent from going to another bake sale.

And just because of one tiny little world-crippling incident, the government wants to come in with a bunch of new rules. They want to make it against the law to put shit in brownies. Not just brownies, but cookies, blondies, cupcakes, muffins—all the baked goods! Do you want a bureaucrat coming between you and your banana-dingleberry-loaf?

Our system is based on Risk—not the board game,[28] the concept. Wall Street can't have regulators peering over their shoulder. It's like when you're trying to pee—if there is somebody watching you, it's harder to do. Just let the Free Market pee, and it will trickle down and warm everybody. And if, eventually, that pee lands in Mrs. Havermeyer's Brownies—well, they'll certainly be moist. Besides, who's going to notice, with all that shit in there.

THINK YOU DON'T KNOW THE FEDERAL RESERVE? DON'T THINK AGAIN!

Think about who's going to do all this regulating: the Fed. Dun-dun-dun! That's right, the shadowy quasi[29]-governmental organization that operates in total secrecy. No one really knows what goes on behind the Federal Reserve's doors. We're *told* that interest rates are set by a 12-member board known as the Federal Open Market Committee. But who are these 12 members,[30] and how many of them have sworn allegiance to sinister cults like the Masons, the Rosicrucians, the Knights Templar, the Illuminati, the Glitterati, or the Sisterhood of the Traveling Pants?

Now, for the first time in the history of as far as I know, I peel back the walls of the mysterious Federal Reserve building. And blow the lid off its dark and shocking secrets!

---

[28] The board games our system is based on are Monopoly and Sorry.
[29] Literally "hunchbacked."
[30] Seriously, who are they? Could somebody Google it?

INSIDE INSIDE THE FED

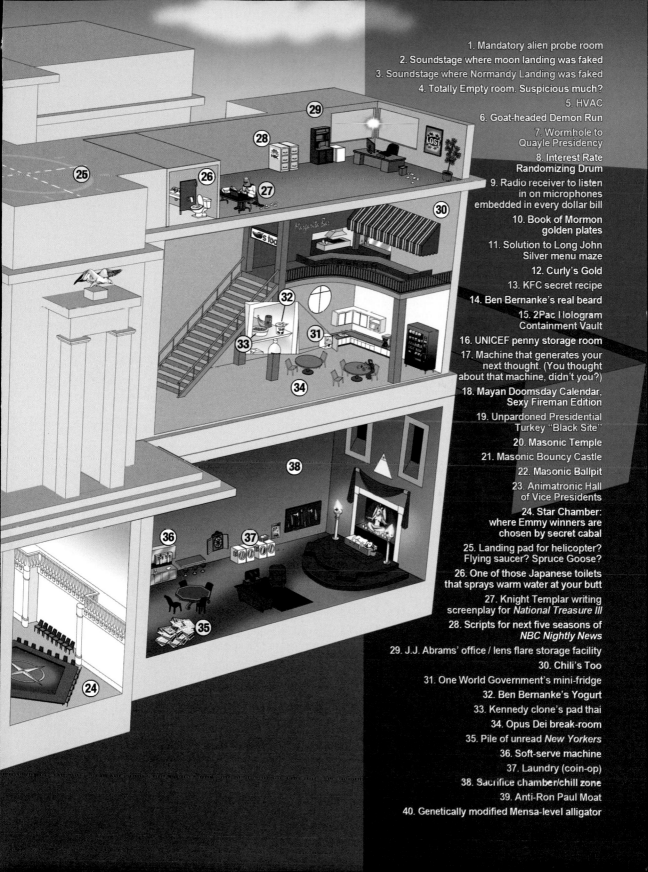

1. Mandatory alien probe room
2. Soundstage where moon landing was faked
3. Soundstage where Normandy Landing was faked
4. Totally Empty room. Suspicious much?
5. HVAC
6. Goat-headed Demon Run
7. Wormhole to Quayle Presidency
8. Interest Rate Randomizing Drum
9. Radio receiver to listen in on microphones embedded in every dollar bill
10. Book of Mormon golden plates
11. Solution to Long John Silver menu maze
12. Curly's Gold
13. KFC secret recipe
14. Ben Bernanke's real beard
15. 2Pac Hologram Containment Vault
16. UNICEF penny storage room
17. Machine that generates your next thought. (You thought about that machine, didn't you?)
18. Mayan Doomsday Calendar, Sexy Fireman Edition
19. Unpardoned Presidential Turkey "Black Site"
20. Masonic Temple
21. Masonic Bouncy Castle
22. Masonic Ballpit
23. Animatronic Hall of Vice Presidents
24. Star Chamber: where Emmy winners are chosen by secret cabal
25. Landing pad for helicopter? Flying saucer? Spruce Goose?
26. One of those Japanese toilets that sprays warm water at your butt
27. Knight Templar writing screenplay for National Treasure III
28. Scripts for next five seasons of NBC Nightly News
29. J.J. Abrams' office / lens flare storage facility
30. Chili's Too
31. One World Government's mini-fridge
32. Ben Bernanke's Yogurt
33. Kennedy clone's pad thai
34. Opus Dei break-room
35. Pile of unread New Yorkers
36. Soft-serve machine
37. Laundry (coin-op)
38. Sacrifice chamber/chill zone
39. Anti-Ron Paul Moat
40. Genetically modified Mensa-level alligator

DOLLAR DAZE

But there's one thing about our dollar that even the Fed can't ruin: its rugged good looks. Reach in your wallet, purse, manpurse, or ladywallet and take out a dollar bill. Give it a good look. I'll bet you a dollar that it's the most beautiful currency you've ever seen. I win—it is. Now send me that dollar.[31]

HEAD OF STATE—NOW WITH 300% MORE HEAD!

Sure, there are slight cosmetic changes every few years. For example, the size of the portraits' heads on the bills has been increased, due to inflation.

But overall, our money has remained the same size, shape, and color for nearly a hundred years. We have resisted incorporating the latest fads, like holograms, or a stable underlying economy.

Still, every few years, complaints get lodged from those who are blind to its beauty. For example, the blind.[32] They argue that bills of the same size and texture make it impossible for them to tell the difference, and that small changes would make it much easier for everybody to use. Oh, really, hypothetical blind person? What about our wallets? We'd have to have a different size wallet for each denomination. How much would that cost us? We love our money just the way it is. That's why we'll never accept the farce of a one dollar coin.

SACAJAWHATNOW?
I CAN'T HAVE A WOMAN'S
HEAD IN MY POCKET.
I'M A MARRIED MAN!

Dollar coins make no sense. They're too bulky and unwieldy. And think about vending machines—if your dollar coin is wrinkled, how are you going to smooth it out?

Most damning to the dollar coin is that they feature women, which, given the current pay scale, means it is only worth 75% as much as a man-dollar.

---

[31] Don't pretend like you don't have one; it's right in your hand.

[32] Note to self: Leave this section out of the audiobook.

WHO'S RIDING OUR BUCKTAILS?

In an attempt to be taken seriously, a lot of joke nations have called their currency a "dollar." Don't be fooled by these cheap knock-offs.

JAMAICAN DOLLAR ▶
SIMILAR TO THE U.S. DOLLAR, EXCEPT THAT IT IS PRINTED ON ROLLING PAPER.

◀ **NEW ZEALAND DOLLAR**
COME ON, MAN, YOU'RE ON THE CURRENCY. THE LEAST YOU CAN DO IS COMB YOUR HAIR!

SINGAPORE DOLLAR ▶
EVEN THE GUY ON THE SINGAPORE DOLLAR IS BORED BY THE SINGAPORE DOLLAR.

◀ **BRUNEI DOLLAR**
IS THIS CURRENCY OR A FEMININE HYGIENE AD?

TAIWANESE DOLLAR ▶
WE GET IT. YOU'VE GOT DIRECT TV. MOVE ON!

◀ **HONG KONG DOLLAR**
DOES ANYONE HAVE CHANGE FOR THE TRAILER TO *TRON 3*?

111

GOLD: THE GOLD STANDARD OF CURRENCY STANDARDS

Book Nation, no one is more passionate about gold than I am. I love gold. Deeply. I'm talking about "climbing a tree outside its window and watching it open Christmas presents with its new boyfriend" kinda love.[33]

I love all forms of gold: Gold coins, gold bars, gold ingots, Golden Grahams, and

BETTY WHITE HAS ONLY CONTINUED TO INCREASE IN VALUE

The Golden Girls! I could go on.

… and I will! Goldilocks, Ari Gold, Goldman Sachs. There. I'm spent.

The quest for gold has driven all of mankind's accomplishments. For instance, gold is the only reason I make a TV show.

Aztec gold is why Spanish conquistadors came to the New World, making them the first Hispanics to take away American jobs. Helpful hint to the exploited peoples of the future: Don't bedeck yourselves in the precious resource that your conquerors are looking for.

WITHOUT THE GOLD, THIS IS AN INSECT-WINGED BARBIE.

BAD MOVE, MONTY.

Gold is the soundest of sound investments. All the smart, long-term money is on Gold. Although if you're really smart, you'll put long-term Gold on Gold. Because any money you put on gold will eventually be worthless. You see, paper money's worth is unreliable. It only has value because we arbitrarily decide it does. But gold

---

[33] I have 25 gold fillings, only three of which were medically necessary. And only 24 of which are in my mouth.

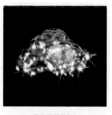

PRETTY!

has intrinsic value because…well…look at it…it's shiny!

And gold has always gone only up in value. Just look at the graph to the right.

Gold's immutable value is why this page has been printed with 100% pure gold leaf, so in an emergency its words can be scraped off, melted down, and used to buy hard tack or women.

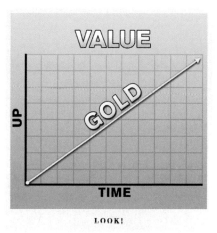

LOOK!

PIRACY WARNING: IF THESE WORDS ARE NOT GOLD COLORED, YOU MAY BE IN POSSESSION OF A BOOTLEG COPY OF THIS BOOK. FURTHERMORE, IF THE LETTERS ON THIS PAGE HAVE TURNED BLACK, THAT INDICATES THAT THEY WERE PRINTED IN CADMIUM, A KNOWN CARCINOGEN, AND THIS IS LIKELY A CHINESE BOOTLEG. HAVE THIS BOOK REMOVED BY A HAZMAT TEAM AND PURCHASE ANOTHER.

THERE'S GOLD IN THEM THAR STANDARDS!

Nation, you can't spell "**g**ood **old** days" without gold. You also can't spell "goat flood" or "gong mold" without it. And there was a time when gold made the American Dollar great. The Greenback used to be gold-backed. But thanks to the paper unions and the presidential-portrait-artists lobby, we went off the gold standard.

Well, no more! I want to go back to a system where I can walk into a Starbucks with a gold ingot and a nutmeg grater and just shave off enough dust for a Venti caramel macchiato. And there's never been a better time to invest in gold. Because we are fast approaching…

THE ARMAGOLDEN [34]

I don't want to alarm you, but we're all going to die soon in a post-apocalyptic Afterland where zombie biker cults seize our malls,[35] and our primary food source is ash.

Imagine this: George Soros and Warren Buffett pull all their money out of the stock market, causing a crash. Just then, China calls in our debt. With the markets in freefall, we don't have enough scratch to pay them back. This causes Europe's economy to implode—first in the brie and schnitzel markets, but it quickly spreads to Greece, and the world is engulfed in Saganaki flames!

NEXT WEDNESDAY

Soon, fuel gangs roam the streets looking for gasoline, which they call "Fire Snapple." Suburban refugees are ruled by leather-clad circus freaks and spikey-haired female slut warriors in tiny leather shorts and tops that expose a fair amount of under-boob![36]

Dogs take over the government! North and South Carolina switch places! VHS tapes are popular again! The Internet ceases to function, and computers are burned for heat—except for the keyboards, which become percussion instruments for mutant jazz musicians, trading a song for a Mason jar of Fire Snapple.

I'm not making this stuff up! I'm imagining it. Especially the part about the spikey-haired slut warrior who, despite her ensemble, is a very tender lover!

So let me ask you this: Do you think your sector's Ur-Lord is going to accept a stack of paper in exchange for a bag of uncontaminated rice seed? No, you need something with tangible value. You can: 1) become a slave in the garbanzo mines of Mexifornia. Or: 2) start investing in gold now and enjoy the sweet life in the Craterscape, enjoying box seats at the Thunderdome, sampling the finest cuts of man tartar, lying around your satin tent from which you rule your spice tribe with your spikey-haired female slut warrior.[37]

The choice is yours.

We'll be right back with more *America Again*, after this word from our sponsor.

---

[34] AKA "The AuPOCALYPSE"

[35] Zombie bikers love Yankee Candle.

[36] But tasteful.

[37] She has a name! It's Brenda.

114

ENERGY

fig 23.3-D. STEPHEN COLBERT

CHAPTER FIVE

ENERGY

"IF YOU LIKE IT, THEN YOU SHOULDA PUT A RIG ON IT."

—*Secretary of Energy Beyoncé Knowles*

Energy is no game. It's a vital part of our economy. But, what if it was a game? We'd be A-Rod, strapped to LeBron's back, being thrown downfield by Tom Brady. We only have 5% of the world's population, yet we use 20% of the energy. We're beating expectations by 400%, according to my diesel-powered calculator!

Point is, we're winning Energy. If you watch TV, and I pray you do, you know that our nation's biggest potential employer is America's Oil and Gas Producers. The reason you know that is a series of powerful energy ads, which prove that the way to get this nation back on track is through coal mining, oil drilling, drill mining, coal oiling, oil milling, drill coaling, and droil mllillning.

Here with more on the exciting opportunities provided by America's Oil and Gas Producers, is the attractively authoritative, yet approachable, blonde woman in a business suit from those ads.

SPECIAL ADVERTORIAL SECTION

Thanks, Stephen. Big fan of you and your work on *The Stephen Colbert Show.*

In today's energy economy, Americans are looking for real solutions. And America's Oil and Gas Producers can bring those solutions, today—and all of tomorrow's todays, tonight. And you can trust me, because I'm walking forward as I say this. Long, confident strides that are a visual metaphor for the strides we need to take as a country.

We are Today's Energy Companies—not your dad's energy company, the one that existed in a statistically corollary but not-proven-to-be-causal relationship with his emphysema.

THANKS TO MY STILETTO HEELS, I'VE STARTED A FEW NEW WELLS ALREADY!

We're forward-thinking, positive, and make generous use of white space because it denotes cleanliness.

DOESN'T THIS LOOK CLEAN?

The fact[1] is: America has some of the greatest energy resources on Earth, which, according to our Guessologists' Hope-jections, if used in combination with technology yet to be invented or imagined, could sustain us for the next 6,000 years. Do you think any other country has those advantages? Think again. Then, think again—about Today's Energy Companies, today. Also: Jobs.

Did you know that in terms of raw supply, the United States is the Saudi Arabia of coal? Or that we're the equivalent of two Saudi Arabias of natural gas? Without our reliance on fossil fuels we would suddenly find ourselves the Saudi Arabia of not comparing ourselves to Saudi Arabia. Then where would we be?[2]

That's why we need an all-of-the-above approach to energy.[3] That means exploiting yesterday's oil and gas reserves today while exploring for tomorrow's energy of the future now. And that approach depends on policies like approving the Keystone XL pipeline to bring between 800,000 and eight hundred thousand barrels of safe, polite, Canadian oil to American refineries. This pipeline would significantly jobs America's energy power security safety. It's common sense.

---

[1] As researched by a completely independent lab we completely fund.

[2] Not Saudi Arabia!

[3] We mean *above* literally. It's time to drill the sky.

And America agrees.

"I AGREE. BECAUSE OF THE CHILDREN!"

"REGULATIONS? ARE YOU SERIOUS?"

"THINGS IS TOUGH ENOUGH AS THEY IS! FUGGETTABOUTIT!"

"GOO GOO GA GAS!"

"IN THIS ECONOMY? COME ON! I'M AFRICAN AMERICAN!"

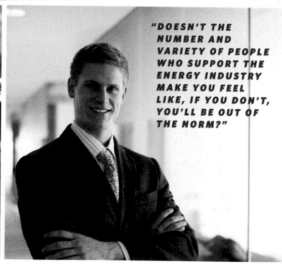

"DOESN'T THE NUMBER AND VARIETY OF PEOPLE WHO SUPPORT THE ENERGY INDUSTRY MAKE YOU FEEL LIKE, IF YOU DON'T, YOU'LL BE OUT OF THE NORM?"

See? It's unanimous. Why aren't you unanimous with us? Together, we can work together to secure America's energy future and create jobs, together.

That's why right here in America, today's energy companies have already begun to jobs tomorrow's energy by leveraging innovation and pioneers we've technologied. Clean future and jobs can work all-of-the-above energy policy future now. As well as future jobs and energy job. Energy future policy jobs, and together the jobs we need to jobs our country forward towards a sunnier and jobbier energy job future. Won't you join us? Job.[4]

---

[4] Job.

Thanks, actress playing someone I can trust!

Book Folks, she's right. Oil powers this country, and it has since the early 1900s. Before that, it was horses.[5]

In 2010 alone, America consumed 6.99 billion barrels of oil. To put that in perspective, if you put 6.99 billion barrels of oil end-to-end, and then painted them all green, and then painted eyes and fangs on the front, it would look like a really long snake.

PULL YOUR WEIGHT, NATURE

There are so many more places we could be drilling for America's future. What

I'VE GOT A SCARY STORY FOR YOU, KIDS: $5 A GALLON! THE END.

would you say if I told you there is an untapped oil reserve on land we're not using right here in America that could drive down the price of gas by a dollar or more overnight?[6] And to get it, all we have to do is let petroleum companies ravage our National Parks! Sadly, a sinister conspiracy is hoarding these resources for themselves. This powerful and shadowy cabal is known as "campers."

And they're not alone. Take the Coastal Elites who don't mind filling their Priuses with oil from flyover states they sneer at, like Texas or Oklawhatever, but when it comes to putting oil platforms off the Capes of their Cod, they claim offshore rigs are *ugly*. Well, if you ask me, they kind of look like the Eiffel Tower. "Oh, please don't put an Eiffel Tower, **one of the**

OIL-LA-LA!

---

[5] And slaves, but let's just focus on the horses.

[6] That night: Sept. 24, 2030.

most photographed buildings in the world, right in front of my house! That would be *too* romantic!"

The enviros whine about how an undersea oil spill might harm their precious man-eating sharks. But that's conveniently overlooking the fact that OFFSHORE DRILLING IS ACTUALLY CLEANING UP A MASSIVE OIL SPILL.

There's an ocean of crude beneath that ocean of ocean—a potential spill that oil companies are working tirelessly to extract before it can escape its containment rock and cause a mega-disaster so destructive we might never recover, no matter how many uplifting Dawn commercials we watched.

IF YOU'RE LOOKING AT THIS, YOU'VE DONE YOUR PART.

But for some reason, you never hear liberal environmentalists talk about all that oil lurking under the seabed. Why is that, guys? ⟶

Folks, there's no time to waste.[7] *We must get that oil out from under the ocean.* Our children swim in there! Or at least they would if they'd put down the damned iPad and enjoy the vacation we blew so much money on![8]

COULD IT BE...
BECAUSE IT'S BLACK???

COAL

Of all the energy sources that will define America's future, none have defined America's past's future more than coal. During the Industrial Revolution, coal was the reason our steamships could travel; the reason our street lamps burned bright; the reason that until 1970, you couldn't see Chicago.

Naturally, the nature-hugging naysayers naysay that we should stop using coal.

But where would America be without coal? Picture a land with no heavy industry, no highways, no skyscrapers, no neon signs visible from space—just acre after

---

[7] For instance, this footnote was completely unnecessary.

[8] Ha! Busted by your own e-book, kids! Now go swimming and leave Daddy to enjoy his Thermos of "special lemonade."

acre of rolling green fields and frolicking wildlife. Smug, frolicking wildlife.

I say we should be proud of our coal, because America is perched on a buttload of it. To be precise: 272 billion buttloads. That's enough to power America for 200 butt-years! And since coal is non-renewable, that means *it will only go up in value*. That's why the kids are so excited about it!

LOOK AT THIS ASSHOLE.

"SANTA BROUGHT US COAL!"

THE NEW COAL:
THIS AIN'T YOUR DADDY'S ANTHRACOSIS

Now, when you hear "coal," you probably think of soot-covered laborers trapped in mineshafts, murdered canaries, and Black Lung. Well, get with the times, Grandpa! Today's coal is safe and modernized, using advanced, state-of-the-art technologies to create a fuel called **"CLEAN COAL."** The process is complex and highly technical, but I've broken it down in the diagram below:

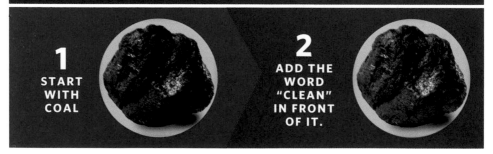

HOW COAL IS CONVERTED INTO *CLEAN* COAL

1 START WITH COAL

2 ADD THE WORD "CLEAN" IN FRONT OF IT.

STEPHEN COLBERT'S DEEPLY PERSONAL ANECDOTE

It is widely known that the same forces that create coal create diamonds, which is why I gave my wife a 5-pound lump of anthracite mounted on a ring when I proposed. I told her it symbolized my commitment—that I would stay with her for the millions of years it would take for that coal to turn into a diamond. In return, she insisted I buy her a real diamond. And as far as she knows, I did.

A REAL COAL WORKER

As great as coal is, too little credit goes to the downtrodden, hardworking Americans who bring it to us: the coal *magnates*. It's about time someone told *their* story. So like Studs Terkel before me, I traveled the country[9] collecting personal accounts of these invisible American workers, that the world might know their plight.

I sat down with Earl in his office suite, the evening sun peeking in through the half-drawn Venetian blinds. For Earl, each word takes effort—a shortness of breath acquired after decades of cigar smoke and brandy.

EARL BRANSON...IN HIS OWN WORDS

Bein' a coal magnate's pretty much all a body can do in these parts. My daddy started workin' this company when he was 14 year old, just like his daddy done.

"NOBODY KNOWS THE TROUBLE I'VE HEARD ABOUT."

CEOin's in the blood, you could say. I'd guess my pappy quit when he was 49 year old. Didn't have much choice. Some man from Washington come and told him they needed him for the lobbyin'. After that, we didn't see him much but for Congressional recess.

I graduated High School back in '68, May. Been workin' at the mine company ever since. It's hard work,

---

[9] Technically, my country club.

but it's honest. I get up about 9, 9:30, put on the suit. But I tell ya, ever' time I take the elevator up that shaft, I'm thinkin', I don't know if I'll be comin' home tonight—'cuz I might knock off in the middle of the afternoon.

'Course, there's been some hard times. Few years back, a mine shaft collapsed. Worst PR disaster this holler ever seen. The whole town got flooded with TV cameras, an' lawyers leached into the local courthouses. Lost some good execs that day.

I always tell my son, "Don't do what your daddy does." 'Cause it ain't right, what they done to us mine magnates. All the regulations, gov'ment come right onto your property, dig through your safety records, make threats. I'd call it quits, but bein' a magnate's all I know. That, and raisin' Arabian horses.

NATURAL GAS:
IT'S PERFECTLY NATURAL. AND PERFECTLY GAS.

Folks, we can't blindly depend on coal forever. If America is going to be energy independent, we need to blindly depend on something else. And for a long time, we had no idea what that could be, no matter how hard we blindly looked for it.

Then came a tale of all-American ingenuity and random geographical happenstance. Because it turns out America is sitting on 482 trillion cubic feet of natural gas! We just stumbled on it! It's like we went down to the basement to dust off the Nordic Track and discovered a Picasso.[10]

MY CHEVY TAHOE GETS 30 MILES PER GUERNICA

---

[10] Also, in this metaphor, we burn Picassos.

The next step was obvious:

PULL MY FINGER!

What will burst out is clean-burning, easy to transport, odorless, quiet, and very, very profitable. In short, it's a big ol' "silent but wealthy." And natural gas is absolutely, 100% safe-ish. All we have to do is make sure we leave enough behind so that the Earth keeps floating in space.

Our gas is trapped in this rock called shale. But we can liberate it using a process called "fracking," or Hydrofracturing for less short. Now, some enviro-worrymentalists say that shattering the bedrock of Pennsylvania into a chemical slurry may not be safe, but Evel Knievel did a lot of things that weren't safe, and he was awesome! I don't recall the EPA ever forcing him to reveal the chemicals in his shattered bones. Checkmate.

But I say, when it comes to decisions that will affect our future, we should leave it up to the future. And I believe that children are the future.

BREAKING RECORDS...AND HIS FEMUR

Kids' Corner

THE FRACKTASTICAL WORLD OF ENERGY INDEPENDENCE!

Children are the ones who will eventually decide where and how we get our energy. And when they grow up, they'll find that you can't run a car on Mountain Dew.[11] So it's important to teach them about securing America's energy independence.

Luckily, kids will believe anything told to them by a cartoon character. One of my favorites was "Talisman Terry, the Friendly Fracosaurus," created back in 2009 by Talisman Energy, America's premiere Canadian hydrofracking company. Unfortunately, there was a public outcry over selling controversial drilling methods to children, and Terry was sent to a farm upstate to become energy for future generations.

But some ideas are too good to let them go extinct.[12] So I've created my own kid-friendly drilling champion to teach our children all of the great things about hydrofracking. Teachers, feel free to make copies of these pages for everyone in your classroom! And then feel compelled to pay me substantial royalties!

---

[11] I found out last week.
[12] I will never give up on you, XFL.

Hi, kids! My name is Tyrannosaurus Frax, but my friends call me T-Frax, and I am a radical prehistoric hydro-fracturing engineer. Cool gnarly! I skatebladed over to tell you about an awesome clean American energy source right here in your neighborhood: Natural Gas!

That's right, I said gas. Faaaarrrrt. Hope you were listening, "Kids' Choice Award for Best Dinosaur Fart" voters! Because there's more where that came from. Gogurt Rules!

But let's get back to natural gas, one of the safest, best energy sources in the whole world. You can use it for, like, a million cool things: heating houses, cooking chicken, making water warm, and even off-the-hook stuff like gas-based commercial desiccant unit cooling systems!

WHEN IS PIXAR GONNA MAKE A MOVIE WHERE THESE FALL IN LOVE?

So you're asking yourself (and prob all your buds on Twitter #totesawesome!), where does natural gas come from? I'll spit it.

Natural gas is made of—get ready for it—me! Well, not me exactly, but all my dinosaur pals and family, who, over millions of years, were compressed by underground heat into a rockin' source of energy. Don't worry. They're cool with it. Even my grandma.

"SAY WHAAA?!"

Thing is, natural gas loves playing hide and seek, and it has found the sweetest hiding spot ever—under the entire earth! That's

132

where hydrofracking companies (like the one your mom or dad could work for) come in. We dig massively deep wells, longer than 5,000 Fruits by the Foot! We "go seek" natural gas by spraying water and chemicals into all the best hiding spots. Tag! You owe me a Hunger Games.

MAJOR WARNING: Some boring NOOB grownups will try to tell you that fracking causes earthquakes. Hellzs to tha nah! All that water and drilling just tickles the Earth!

They'll also try to rap at ya that the chemicals we spray down the wells could get into the groundwater. But who wants to drink something called *ground*water in the first place? Grody! You know what I call water that's had chemicals added to it by a big company? Sprite!

Hey, know what's cool? Dragons. I know, because I'm a dinosaur. We hang all the time. And you can hang with one, too, right in your kitchen. Because sometimes that fracked gas seeps into the water supply and blasts out of your faucet. *Whoa,* did your dragon just fire-breathe all over the dishes?!

HEY, KIDS! LET'S WASH SOME MARSHMALLOWS!

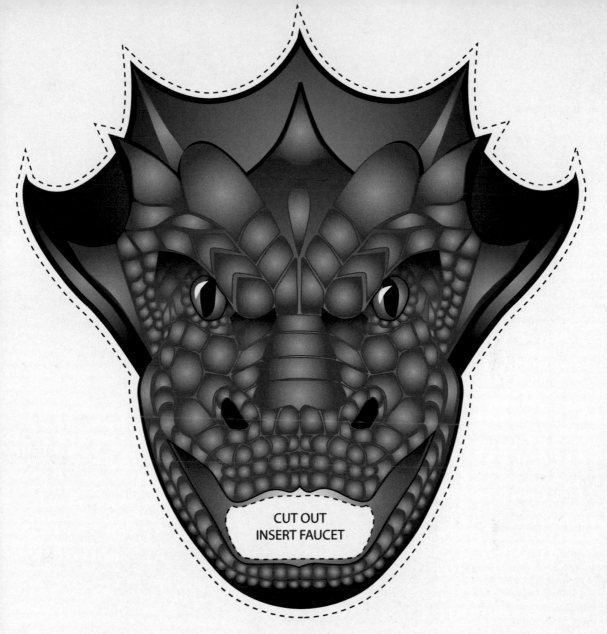

CUT OUT
INSERT FAUCET

HEY DUDES AND LADYDUDES, JUST
CUT OUT THIS SA-*WEEEET* DRAGON
FACE AND TURN YOUR FAUCET INTO
A FIRE-BREATHING BEAST OF YORE!

CAUTION: CUT-OUT IS HIGHLY FLAMMABLE

Well, I wish I could keep hangin' with you dudes, but I have to shimmy. It's getting near my curfew, and I've got a whole lot more gas to release.

Faaarrrt! Oh man. I did it again! Adios, homeskillets!

Remember...he who smelt it, ensured America's Energy Independence!

★ ATTENTION DOWNTRODDEN READER! UTOPIA AWAITS! ★

What if I told you there was a place in America that's full of endless opportunity, a place with nearly zero unemployment, a place where everyone can get a job, a place where the starting salary is six figures, a place where the rivers run with whiskey, a place where hot young women hang from the trees like ripe fruit, a place where all of that is true except those last 2 things? [13]

It's a land called North Dakota. The whole state is perched on an oil and gas deposit called "The Bakken Formation," which is oozing with 200,000 square miles of sweet crude—and that means jobs, jobs, jobs! So if you want opportunity, Go West, Young Man…Then Hang A Right And Go North Until You Can't Feel Your Toes, Young Man!

Now, the only problem with the North Dakota oil rush is that the state's infrastructure is presently set up to handle only the pre-oil-boom population of Bart.

So the rental market is a little tight. You have the choice of living in your car or in something called "MAN CAMPS." [14]

BART: HIGH SCHOOL VALEDICTORIAN *AND* LEAST LIKELY TO SUCCEED

"YOU ALL GOT A DOG I COULD CRAWL INSIDE?"

MAN CAMP! WHERE ACTIVITIES INCLUDE STARING AND YEARNING!

---

[13] Also, no trees.

[14] Note: Do not rent the DVD *Man Camp*. It is not an orientation video.

These makeshift metroplexes have been thoughtfully assembled by the oil companies from old shipping containers. Now working men can live comfortably in a space that once transported contraband livestock, industrial solvents, or illegal immigrants hoping for a better life living in a shipping container.

North Dakota's Man Camps have it all: Work! Salaries! Bunkmates! Shared showers! High winds! No women! A DVD player! Unlimited masturbation! Shuttle buses!

And for those craving excitement, the options are as endless as the highway. Just hundreds of miles away is the relatively resort state of *South* Dakota!

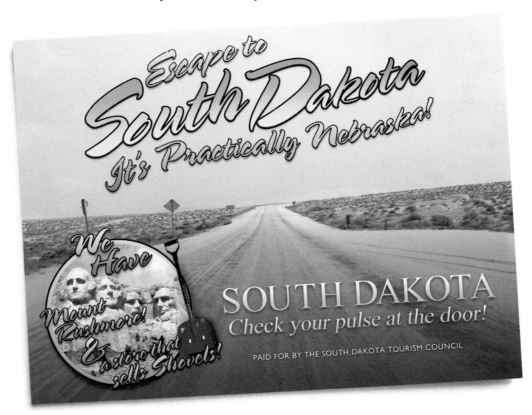

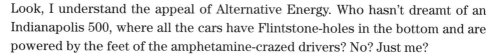

ALTERNATIVE ENERGY:
DON'T CHANGE SOURCES MID-SCHEME

Look, I understand the appeal of Alternative Energy. Who hasn't dreamt of an Indianapolis 500, where all the cars have Flintstone-holes in the bottom and are powered by the feet of the amphetamine-crazed drivers? No? Just me?

Still, as I write this, there's no alternative source that can hold a candle to fossil fuels.[15] That's why I'm for an "All of the Above" energy policy, as long as it includes none of the below:

SOLAR POWER

Harnessing the sun's power may seem like a good idea, but only if you're delirious with sunstroke. It's completely impractical—how are you going to fit the entire sun in your car? It's huge and super-hot. You'd use up most of the power running the air conditioning.

And Lunar Power is just as impractical. If we want energy powered by the moon, we'd have to put a bunch of werewolves in giant hamster wheels, but that would work only once a month!

NOT A REALISTIC SOLUTION.

TIDAL POWER

Some scientists think we can get our energy from ocean tides because they're more reliable than wind or sunlight. Oh, really? How can you count on something that gets high twice a day?

ALGAE

Algae? I don't trust it. First of all, look at how it's spelled. And don't tell me that algae contains up to 50% lipid oil, because I have no idea what lipid oil is. Besides, if algae is such a great source of energy, how come my car stopped working when I drove it into my koi pond?

---

[15] Warning: do not hold a candle to fossil fuels.

WIND POWER

Wind is for powering your sailboat when your motor fails and for making our flags flutter majestically. Period.

People who advocate for wind power have never asked the obvious question. What happens when one of these wind farms has an accident and we're faced with a massive wind spill? Have you ever tried getting wind out of the air? It's nearly impossible!

THINK OF ALL THE POOR BIRDS COVERED IN THIS STUFF.

GEOTHERMAL ENERGY

Geothermal energy is power generated inside the earth. Before we can harness geothermal power, we have to take the planet's temperature with a geothermometer. And I have no idea where the Earth's rectum is![16]

The most common type of geothermal power plant uses heated water from under the earth's crust to generate electricity. Really? You don't think maybe the mole-people are going to notice a sudden drop in their water pressure?

"GAAAHH?! WHO FLUSHED THE TOILET?!"

MORE OIL: WHAT A GREAT ALTERNATIVE!

Hey, the earth isn't broken yet. Why fix it? That's why the best alternative to oil is more oil. More oil is different than our normal oil because there's more of it. More oil is by far the best answer to our oil problems. After all, if you fight fire with fire, why not fight oil with oil? With more oil, the oil industry could make more money to invest in cleaner oil refineries and safer oil rigs and better clean-up services. The possibilities—like our oil supply—are endless! And the oil industry solemnly swears that it will keep working on the alternative energy of more oil until it has perfected it.

---

[16] Windsor, Canada?

GLOBAL WARMING

These days it seems like you can't go out on a scorching December morning, help your children build a soilman, and enjoy a refreshing glass of iced cocoa, without hearing some liberal alarmist complain about "Global Warming."

IT'LL NEVER LAST

Yes, everywhere you turn, you hear members of the enviro-stapo screaming "Greenhouse Gases!" and "Carbon Footprints!" and "Has anyone seen Key West lately?" Their answer to this made-up problem is to burn less fossil fuel. But Nation, what these eco-maniacs don't know could fill the hole in the ozone layer, which also doesn't exist.

When it comes to climate change, the Science just isn't in yet. Trust me. Every day I check my mailbox to see if the Science is in, and every day, no Science.[17]

I'm so sick of info-fondling lefties saying they already have the data. Sorry, but

CRANK THAT CO$_2$
UP TO CO$_{11}$!

a few ice core samples and a 0.2 degree temperature spike in Ottawa doesn't prove crap. You want science? Let's do some real science! Let's put on our lab coats, but no lab pants—because when I do the scientific method, I go balls to the wall.[18]

There's only one way to bring the science in once and for all. All the nations of the world sign a treaty agreeing to jack their carbon footprint through the roof.

Once the results of the experiment are in, then we'll finally know for sure whether we shouldn't have done what we just did.

Then and only then will I buy one of those squiggly light bulbs. But only for the garage! I look like a gargoyle under fluorescents.

INCANDESCENT

FLUORESCENT

---

[17] Just dozens of Pottery Barn catalogs that used to be Brazilian rainforest.

[18] Same way I do the rhythm method.

Oh, hello! I was just posing for another *National Geographic* spread. Something about *America's Coastal Devastation* or some shit like that. Wasn't really paying attention.

Still I'm glad you're here. You see, there's been a lot of talk about the environmental impact of our friendly neighborhood oil rig exploding. Well, I think it's time I shared the wildlife's perspective on this "ecological catastrophe." Speaking personally—I'm rich! *Rich, motherfuckers*! Who has two wings and is rolling six-deep in black gold? This pelican, that's who!

Now that I'm coated from beak to bunghole in precious crude, it's gonna be nothing but the high life for me. For starters, no more migrating, chumps. I'm gonna be straight-kickin' it in business class. No one hands you champagne and a hot towel when you're humpin' it solo. And you definitely don't get to watch *27 Dresses* starring Katherine Heigl. Man, what I'd give to incubate her eggs.

And folks, I'm not the only one making out like an oil-slathered bandit. You see that egret over there? The one flopping in the tar? He's about to make an offer to buy the Dallas Mavericks.

Best of all, I'll finally be able to afford rhinoplasty—that's right, a beak reduction. I'm thinking I'd look cute with Zac Efron's nose. And maybe some calf implants.

Shit! Here come the Greenpeace volunteers and their little toothbrushes. SCRAM! This oil is mine, you damn hippies! MINE!

Now if you'll excuse me, it's mating season, and thanks to my sugar daddies in the petroleum industry, I'm about to drill, baby, drill!

ELECTIONS

fig 24.3-D. **STEPHEN COLBERT**

CHAPTER SIX

ELECTIONS

"I REGRET I HAVE BUT $25 TO DONATE TO YOUR CAMPAIGN."

—Nathan Hale to
John Adams' robo-courier

The rustle of the voting booth curtain. The musty aroma of the elderly volunteers. The hushed oaths of the guy jimmying open the voting machine with his belt buckle. And through it all, the majestic bunt of the bunting. It's Election Day, and Americans from all walks of life are eagerly lining up to ask their bosses for an unpaid afternoon off to vote.

On that hallowed Tuesday[1] in November, each and every citizen plays their part in America's grand democratic experiment. And when the polls close, cable news' professional opinionizers analyze the results for us, thoughtfully stroking their chins and, if their side is winning, other parts.

To the north, the control group Canada has begun to suspect that their whole country is a placebo.

But whoever takes the election, the winner is clear: America. Because our elections are a massive job-creating industry—one of the few we have left. You see, there was a time in America when we made things. Large, loud, shiny things. Things that went "vroom-vroom," "clang-clang,"

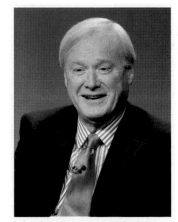

HANDS WHERE I CAN SEE 'EM, MATTHEWS.

---

[1] Tuesday where I live. In most poor and minority neighborhoods, I think it's Wednesday. Check your local GOP windshield flyers.

and "vfrrit-vfrrit-vfrrit."[2] But the steelworks closed, the tool and die shops went overseas, the textile mills shuttered, and the shutter factories Venetian-blinded.

But our vote factories are still churning out a steady stream of freshly combed candidates ready to kiss your baby and get their photo taken with the elusive Elderly Gay NASCAR Latina Soccer Veteran.

By the end of the 2012 elections, our Electoral Industrial Complex will have spent nine billion dollars—through local ad buys, bus sides, rally confetti, lawn signs, slogan-coining, teeth-whitening, spray-tanning, and jowl-fluffing.

While a thriving sector of our economy, American politics are not yet an export industry. For the time being, most of our politics are bought and consumed solely in America. Much like our sitcoms.

30 ROCK, OR AS IT WAS KNOWN DURING ITS BRIEF RUN IN KOREA, SPINSTER COTTON PANTIES

GIRLFRIEND, PLEASE… YOU THINK THIS MUCH NECK JUST *HAPPENS?!*

All that money means good jobs for pollsters, speech writers, marketing gurus, social media coordinators, opposition researchers, advertising directors, strategic consultants, image wranglers, and mistress containment squads.

For instance, if a candidate doesn't have any Hispanic friends,[3] he can hire someone who does. That's where ethnic targeting consultants come in, helping campaigns with everything from messaging to teaching your guy how to really milk the double "R" in "burrito"—you never know when you'll be within earshot of that Elderly Gay NASCAR Latina Soccer Veteran.

Last but least, there are the campaign volunteers, who are not paid, but nonetheless go through an unbelievable amount of Chex Mix.[4]

CHEWED THROUGH HER CHAINS!

---

[2] Corduroy pants, obviously.

[3] Does making eye contact with a busboy count?

[4] Note to campaigns: the kind without nuts is cheaper.

So where does all that money come from? I'm glad you asked.

TOGETHER, WE CAN DO SOMETHING

By purchasing this book, you have agreed to receive fundraising emails. If you would like to be removed from the email list, simply travel back in time and un-purchase this book.[5]

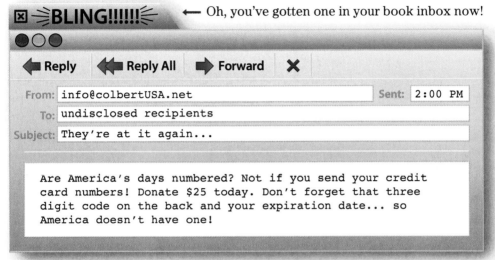

⌧ ≶BLING!!!!!!≶   ← Oh, you've gotten one in your book inbox now!

◉◯◯

◀ **Reply**   ◀◀ **Reply All**   ▶ **Forward**   ✖

From: info@colbertUSA.net   Sent: 2:00 PM

To: undisclosed recipients

Subject: They're at it again...

Are America's days numbered? Not if you send your credit card numbers! Donate $25 today. Don't forget that three digit code on the back and your expiration date... so America doesn't have one!

SMALL DONORS

You see, if you want to win Democracy, the **big money** is in **small donors.** Herman Cain understood that.

A great man once said:

SOMEONE'S TALKING ABOUT ME?
AND LOOKING AT ME?
AWWWW, SHUCKY DUCKY!

"There are no small donors, only small donations you get from spamming people until you catch them reading emails drunk."

—A Great Man

It's a statement that's as true today as it was the day I made it up. [6]

---

[5] Also, time permitting, kill Hitler. Or at least compliment his painting.

[6] Which is also today.

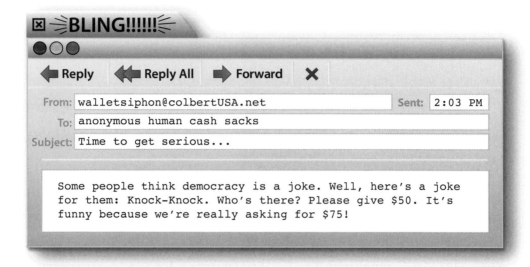

☒ BLING!!!!!!

● ◯ ◯

⬅ Reply   ⬅ Reply All   ➡ Forward   ✖

From: walletsiphon@colbertUSA.net   Sent: 2:03 PM

To: anonymous human cash sacks

Subject: Time to get serious...

Some people think democracy is a joke. Well, here's a joke for them: Knock-Knock. Who's there? Please give $50. It's funny because we're really asking for $75!

In 2008, Barack Obama raised *$750 million*, and *80%* of it came from people who gave *less than 200 bucks*. Now, I just swarmed you with a lot of italicized numbers,

so as a palate-cleanser, I've included a picture of a kindly old man playing the accordion.

That guy is just the type of friendly grandpa who'll toss your campaign a $5 check, no questions asked. Those can add up.[7] And much like with your real grandpa, the way to keep the checks rolling in is to maintain the **appearance of a personal relationship**. Which reminds me:

Hi, Pee-pop! Thanks for reading my book! Did you hear that noise? It's probably me calling to thank you for last year's birthday gift. Just in time for *this* year's birthday! Hope to hear from you soon!

That phone call I just convinced him I made? That's the kind of personal touch small donors respond to. So find a compassionate email-bot to send them.

---

[7] *In multiples of 5!* (More italicized numbers. Go back to the accordion picture.)

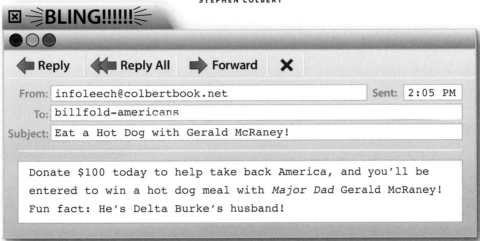

⊠ ≷BLING!!!!!!≷

← Reply   ← Reply All   → Forward   ✕

From: infoleech@colbertbook.net   Sent: 2:05 PM
To: billfold-americans
Subject: Eat a Hot Dog with Gerald McRaney!

Donate $100 today to help take back America, and you'll be
entered to win a hot dog meal with *Major Dad* Gerald McRaney!
Fun fact: He's Delta Burke's husband!

And keep sending them. I'm talkin' more solicitations than an Azerbaijani boner pill spammer.[8] And the best part about fundraising emails? They're just a click away from the "donate" button on your **website**. Speaking of which:

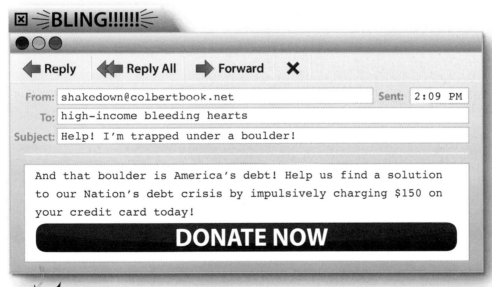

⊠ ≷BLING!!!!!!≷

← Reply   ← Reply All   → Forward   ✕

From: shakedown@colbertbook.net   Sent: 2:09 PM
To: high-income bleeding hearts
Subject: Help! I'm trapped under a boulder!

And that boulder is America's debt! Help us find a solution
to our Nation's debt crisis by impulsively charging $150 on
your credit card today!

DONATE NOW

SPEAK SOFTLY AND CARRY SOME BIG RED

TRUTH PUNCH

Don't forget the most important tool in your small donor toolkit: a stick with a piece of chewed gum on the end you can use to fish dimes out of street grates. Or, more gum!

---

[8] Wazzup, Volum3Spl@sh? I gave you my Amex number. Where's my MaxGirth2000?

Plus, small donors are ne
just relax. This isn't like
desk lamp was ordering
thanks to a different po
the recent Citizens Unite

I
sp
b
W
co
n
y

F

great.
like n

Whoa
tered
feel li

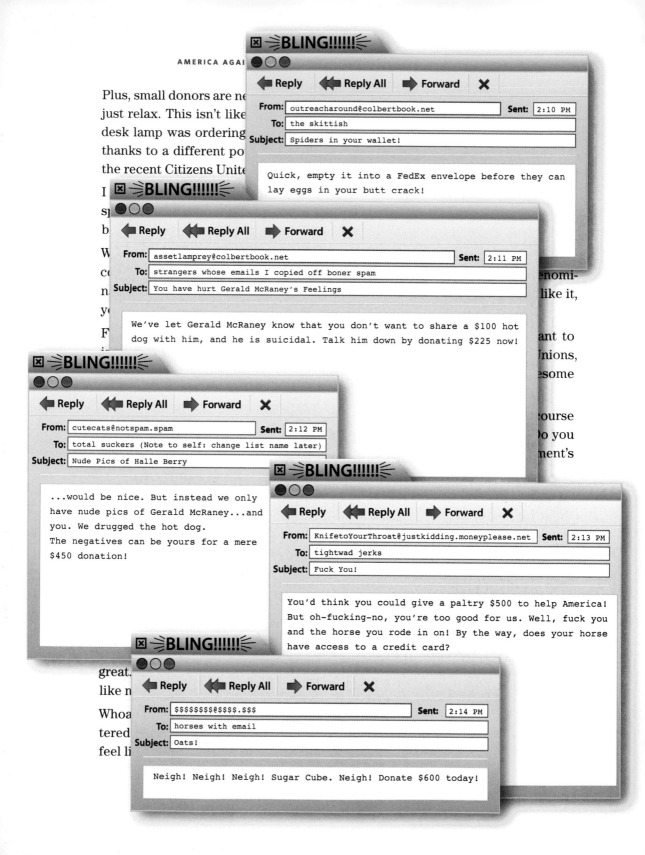

BLING!!!!!!

From: outreacharound@colbertbook.net Sent: 2:10 PM
To: the skittish
Subject: Spiders in your wallet!

Quick, empty it into a FedEx envelope before they can lay eggs in your butt crack!

BLING!!!!!!

From: assetlamprey@colbertbook.net Sent: 2:11 PM
To: strangers whose emails I copied off boner spam
Subject: You have hurt Gerald McRaney's Feelings

We've let Gerald McRaney know that you don't want to share a $100 hot dog with him, and he is suicidal. Talk him down by donating $225 now!

BLING!!!!!!

From: cutecats@notspam.spam Sent: 2:12 PM
To: total suckers (Note to self: change list name later)
Subject: Nude Pics of Halle Berry

...would be nice. But instead we only have nude pics of Gerald McRaney...and you. We drugged the hot dog.
The negatives can be yours for a mere $450 donation!

BLING!!!!!!

From: KnifetoYourThroat@justkidding.moneyplease.net Sent: 2:13 PM
To: tightwad jerks
Subject: Fuck You!

You'd think you could give a paltry $500 to help America! But oh-fucking-no, you're too good for us. Well, fuck you and the horse you rode in on! By the way, does your horse have access to a credit card?

BLING!!!!!!

From: $$$$$$$$@$$$$.$$$ Sent: 2:14 PM
To: horses with email
Subject: Oats!

Neigh! Neigh! Neigh! Sugar Cube. Neigh! Donate $600 today!

But small donors might not be right for everybody. Maybe you don't have the time to commit to fundraising, or maybe you lack the ground resources, or maybe you're just completely unappealing to every person you come in contact with.

Well, you're in luck! There's a simpler answer:

LARGE DONORS

So how do you find big donors? That's a good question, I'm glad I pretended you asked it. Unfortunately, if you don't know large donors already, there's no way you're going to meet

"THIS IS FUN! I DIDN'T KNOW NAPKINS COULD BE MADE OUT OF PAPER!"

them. They got rich avoiding people like you. Big donors are a lot like the secret fight club underneath Frontierland at Disney World. If you don't already know how to get in, nobody's going to tell you. And if you keep pressing, eventually, you're going to wake up hot-glued inside a Goofy costume, fighting for your life with a length of chain.

KICK HIM IN THE EPCOTS!

153

Of course, if you do know rich people, you can't just send them the same mass solicitians you send the groundlings. No, like having sex in a car, crafting large donor emails is an art—one wrong move and suddenly the campaign is in neutral, drifting toward a Sunglass Hut.

Ahem   ← Let an expert show you how it's done.

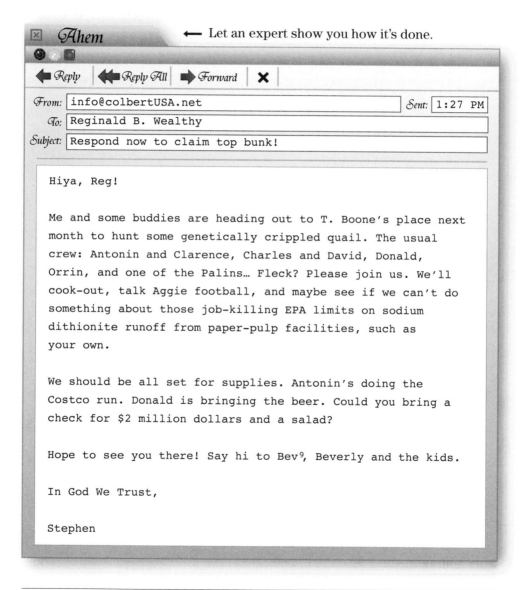

From: info@colbertUSA.net   **Sent:** 1:27 PM
To: Reginald B. Wealthy
Subject: Respond now to claim top bunk!

Hiya, Reg!

Me and some buddies are heading out to T. Boone's place next month to hunt some genetically crippled quail. The usual crew: Antonin and Clarence, Charles and David, Donald, Orrin, and one of the Palins… Fleck? Please join us. We'll cook-out, talk Aggie football, and maybe see if we can't do something about those job-killing EPA limits on sodium dithionite runoff from paper-pulp facilities, such as your own.

We should be all set for supplies. Antonin's doing the Costco run. Donald is bringing the beer. Could you bring a check for $2 million dollars and a salad?

Hope to see you there! Say hi to Bev[9], Beverly and the kids.

In God We Trust,

Stephen

---

[9] Pro-tip: If you are having an affair, insist that your lover legally change his/her name to your spouse's. You'll never gasp out the wrong one.

FUND-RAISING FUN TIP — Ask donors to write their beliefs in the memo line of the check. It will be easier to remember later.

Point is, this election year, large donors are more important than ever, thanks to...

CITIZENS UNITED

Imagine a small town is holding an election. Now, imagine the town has 100 people, 99 of whom each has one apple. Now imagine one man in town, all by himself, has 100 apples. Now, forget all that, because the multi-national apple conglomerate, CoreCorp, has billions of dollars. And these days it can spend it on political ads, thanks to the men, women, and giant well-worn baseball glove of the Supreme Court.[10]

Let me take you back to an historic day: January 21, 2010. The Court was set to rule on *Citizens United v. FEC*, a landmark civil rights case. Once again the Court had a chance to transcend public opinion and extend long-denied rights to a marginal-

YOU CAN CUT THE SEXUAL TENSION WITH A KNIFE.

ized group, as they had in *Brown v. Board of Education*, *Cooper v. Aaron*, and *Third Thing v. Another Black Guy*. Previous courts had brought equality to African Americans, protected women, said it was okay for there to be Latinos, and freed the Gays to engage in what they thoughtfully reminded them was, in fact, sodomy. By 2010, there was only one oppressed minority left in the United States: **Corporations**. And *Citizens United v. FEC* would determine whether these brave Americans would continue to be dehumanized merely because they were not human.

The weight of history was on the Court's shoulders.[11] The decision came down:

---

[10] Anthony Kennedy's legendary jurisprudence is maintained by having clerks rub him with neatsfoot oil and press him under a mattress to keep him supple between cases.

[11] Tends to make Scalia's shoulder hair itch.

The Court ruled that Corporations were people with the First Amendment right to Freedom of Speech, and that money is speech, therefore corporations have the right to the unlimited use of money in political speech.

When I heard the ruling, I was so moved, I gathered my loved ones, and I said, "  ." You can quote me on that. Because I have always believed that money is speech. I may not agree with what you pay, but I'll fight to the death for your right to pay me to agree with you.

THE SUPREME COURT BUILDING FEATURES A STUNNING MARBLE FACADE AND AN IMPOSING SERIES OF STEPS WHICH CONVEY THE MESSAGE, "THE EVENTS THAT OCCUR WITHIN ARE OF THE UTMOST IMPORTANCE TO AMERICA" AS WELL AS THE LESS SUBTLE MESSAGE, "THIS BUILDING IS NOT HANDICAPPED ACCESSIBLE."

CONTEXT, IF YOU INSIST

The details of *Citizens United v. FEC* are irrelevant. However, I will provide them for my Texan readers, who are using this as a high school history textbook. In 2008, a nonprofit corporation called Citizens United wanted to air a film critical of Hillary Clinton titled *Hillary: The Movie*. It was a classic story: boy-meets-girl, girl-murders-Vince Foster. When Citizens United attempted to buy TV ads to promote the movie, the federal government found them to be in violation of the McCain-Feingold Campaign Reform Act, which, as written by John McCain, mandated that only *Matlock* be shown on television during elections. The Supreme Court ruled that placing limits on Citizens United's political spending had violated the corporation's first amendment rights.

Unfortunately, *Hillary: The Movie* never aired. It was later rewritten and released as *Final Destination 4*.

The five men in the majority opinion in *Citizens United* are responsible for **the pinnacle achievement of our democracy**. But if you disagree, you're free to vote against their lifetime appointments.

PEOPLE

Now, the politically naïve might ask, "Doesn't unlimited corporate and union money have the potential to corrupt our electoral system?" I'll pause now so you can say it out loud.[12] Do you hear how foolish you sound? You're talking to a book!

Well, the Supreme Court is way ahead of you. As Justice Kennedy wrote in his majority opinion:

> *"We now conclude that independent expenditures, including those made by corporations, do not give rise to corruption or the appearance of corruption."*
>
> —AN ACTUAL QUOTE

There! Concluded! A smart guy said it. **Independent corporate expenditures do not give rise to corruption.** In fact, they don't even give rise to the *appearance* of corruption. Like the old sayings go: "Tit for nothing," "You scratch my back; my back is scratched," "Quid pro goodness of my heart," and "One hand washes itself while the other hand also washes itself."

Plus, the *Citzens United* ruling **forbids** unlimited donations directly to candidates, which means there's no way a candidate could ever find out if a corporation wants to influence his or her positions. Instead, unlimited donations must take

---

12 This is the pause.

place behind an impenetrable corruption-proof barrier, known as …

Super PACs, AKA Independent, Expenditure-only Political Action Committees bring the unlimited voice of corporate peoples to our elections, one primary-swamping donation at a time.

But, of course, to exercise that much power, Super PACs must adhere to a long list of Rule.

1. Candidates may not coordinate with SuperPACs.

2. How do you keep Microsoft Word from giving you another number when you hit return? There's only one rule.

3. God Dammit, Monica! It won't stop! Get in here!

Okay. Where was I? Oh yeah…

So what counts as coordination? To help you sail the shoals of Election Law, I've put together this handy Super PAC Safety Guide.

Make no mistake, folks, the Federal Election Commission is a serious law enforcement agency. Need proof? Campaigns are so terrified of the FEC that **no one has ever gone to jail for violating an FEC rule.** That's less than the DEA, the FBI, and the IRS *combined*!

So tear out the following laminated chart* and carry it with you on the campaign to keep you out of FEC prison (which I believe is on the southern tip of Asgard).

SUPER PAC COORDINATION
SAFETY GUIDE

OFFICIAL CAMPAIGN/SUPER PAC DOs AND DON'Ts

ILLEGAL COORDINATION

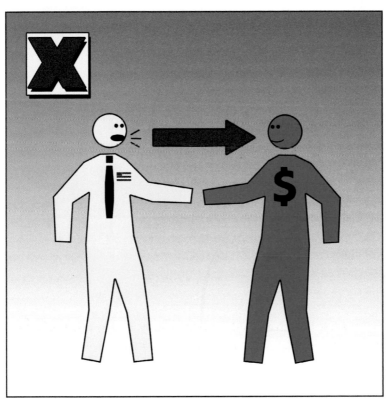

● Candidate telling Super Pac his plans, strategy, or needs

---

* Note to publisher: Do not forget to laminate this page and perforate the edge for easy tearing. Again, THIS IS VERY IMPORTANT TO ME.

LEGAL NON-COORDINATION

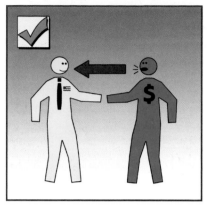

- Super Pac telling candidate its plans, strategies, or needs

- Watching the candidate explain his campaign's plans, strategies, and needs on TV

- Co-owning a private island

- Exploring the Marianas Trench

- Getting married

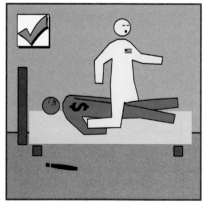

- Doin' it wild style

NOW WHAT?

Once you're rolling in unlimited corporate dough, what should your Super PAC spend it on? Well, there are a lot of good options. First, there are **negative ads**. But if that's against your principles, there are always attack ads. And of course, there are also ads that are scathing indictments, vicious smears, vindictive slanders, heartless curbstomps, relentless disembowelments, sociopathic hitjobs, and positive ads. I would avoid the positive ads. They can seem a little desperate.

Now if we're talkin' negative ads, I love the classics. Lyndon Johnson's "Daisy" ad, which informed voters of Barry Goldwater's love of nuking little girls.

Horton Received 10 Weekend Passes From Prison

◀ Or George H.W. Bush's "Willie Horton" ad, which celebrated Michael Dukakis' fetish for watching murdererous black men go through revolving doors.

And the granddaddy of them all: Woodrow Wilson's landmark "Dancing Snack" ad that undermined the public's trust in the morbidly obese William Howard Taft.

"LET'S ALL GO TO THE LOBBY/LET'S ALL GO
TO THE LOBBY/LET'S ALL GO TO THE LOBBY/
BEFORE TAFT GETS THERE FIRST!"

And the negativity need not stop with ads. Who could forget the effective whisper campaign from 2000 that accused John McCain of having an illegitimate black baby? Or the slightly less effective rumor that he had illegitimate black parents?

And Reader Nation, as the CEO and Chief Title Giver of my own Super PAC, I believe that negative advertising is the most effective way to make clear distinctions not just in politics, but between you and any opponent. So if you're reading this at the bookstore, deciding whether to buy *America Again*, you might be interested in knowing a few things

LIONEL AND BERNICE MCCAIN? *YOU DECIDE.*

about my publishing competition. After all, don't you deserve the bestseller that's right for America?

BOOK	WHY IT'S WRONG FOR AMERICA
	THE CATCHER IN THE RYE He's a phony with a pro-hooker agenda.
	CURIOUS GEORGE Did you know he was "Bi-curious George" in college?
	JAMES AND THE GIANT PEACH A chilling endorsement of Man-Fruit Marriage.
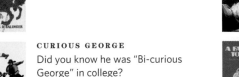	**THE ADVENTURES OF HUCKLEBERRY FINN** Uses the N word.

BOOK	WHY IT'S WRONG FOR AMERICA
	PRIDE AND PREJUDICE Someone's awfully proud of how much she hates Puerto Ricans.
	A FAREWELL TO ARMS You hear that, folks? This book wants to take your guns away!
	THE UGLY DUCKLING A duckling? Sounds like Mr. Swan's been gettin' some pond strange on the side.
	WINNIE THE POOH Uses the T Word.

The choice is yours...

HAPPY ENDING

Of course, there is the slim chance that your Super PAC's candidate doesn't get elected. Maybe their message didn't resonate; maybe it was an off-year election and the base wasn't energized; maybe that whole "naked pistol-waving breakdown in a Santa Monica traffic circle" thing got taken out of context.[13]

"FEED ME!"

Well, don't sweat it. Just because the election is over, doesn't mean you have to give up on what inspired you to start a Super PAC in the first place: Money. You can use your remaining cash however you please! Hire Sarah Palin's relatives as "consultants." Buy clothes for Sarah Palin. Pay for hotel rooms for Sarah Palin. Off the top of my head, I can think of at least one Sarah Palin who's done very well for herself that way.[14]

UNAMERICAN ACTIVITIES

Turns out, other countries have elections, too. I don't recommend them.

Sorry, parliamentary systems, but God created elections to be between one Republican and one Democrat, not your freaky five-ways. If you toss a bunch of extra parties in there, who knows where they stuff their ballots?

HORSE LATER
"ATE SOME BAD SUSHI"

Here's a look at why other countries' elections are just pre-op America impersonators:

RUSSIA: The Russian electoral system works like this: you are given the option of voting for Vladimir Putin or one of several Putin-sanctioned opponents. You are then poisoned by Vladimir Putin.

ENGLAND: In this supposed democracy, Queen Elizabeth has managed to win every election since 1952. Plus, at any time, Parliament can pass a resolution of "no confidence" and dissolve the government. May I remind you, this was also the plot of the most boring *Star Wars*.

CANADA: With their laws mandating use of both French and English, candidates are forced to both kiss babies and French kiss babies. No, thanks.

---

[13] He was just dehydrated!

[14] Hi Sarah! See you at this year's SarahPAC Aerial Wolf "Ho-Down 'n' Mow-Down" Benefit Jamboree!

INDIA: The debates are impossible to follow and last nine hours due to the elaborate dance numbers. Also the losing candidate is reincarnated as tandoori chicken.

"I'LL HAVE INDIRA GANDHI WITH JASMINE RICE."

MEXICO: Leading candidates debate how they will fix Mexico's economy and fight the drug cartels. Those people are then assassinated by the Zetas, and the candidate with the most remaining head is declared the winner.

GERMANY: Germans pride themselves on holding sober, thoughtful, carefully deliberated elections, except for that one time.

THE NETHERLANDS: Dutch elections are frequently rocked by a so-called "June Surprise," when one of the candidates is caught not visiting a prostitute.

ISRAEL: There's no greater friend of Israel's electoral system than yours truly. I stand by the Israeli people's sovereign right to choose leaders that ingather the Jews to the Holy Land, thus hastening its annihilation during the Tribulations that herald the Rapture and the return of Christ.

So, good system, though I gotta say, when you're surrounded by enemies, who has a Defense Minister with one eye?

JAPAN: The Japanese electoral process is tremendously entertaining. A rotting fish is strapped to the candidates' groins, then they are set adrift in a 7,000-gallon water tank filled with eels on PCP. The winner is chosen by the laughing man in the corner of the TV screen. After inauguration, the new prime minister transforms into a 50-foot robot lion that lays fiery waste to Hokkaido.

ARRR! BATTEN DOWN THE HUMMUS!

WHO FRAUDED?

So clearly we have the best electoral system in the world, but as perfect as it is, it is deeply flawed. First of all, did you know that many voting booths have no hook to hang up your pants? I found that out the hard way. But even more disturbing, sometimes **The Guy I Voted For** doesn't win.

Take 2008. I didn't vote for Barack Obama. None of my friends at the club voted for Barack Obama. Nobody I know that is willing to discuss politics with me voted for Barack Obama.

So how did he win? There are only two possible explanations: One, I'm out of step with the majority of my fellow citizens. But that's ridiculous, because I correctly voted for five of the last nine *American Idol* winners. Even a black one!

Which brings me to the only other possible explanation:

I WANNA SAY...FANTA?

VOTER FRAUD!

CRIME SCENE

I know it's shocking—the thought of someone lying to get an "I Voted" sticker made me so sick, I could barely finish the Lorna Doones I stole from the table in front of the blood drive.

But the facts speak for themselves: In Ohio in 2004, out of the 9 million votes cast, *four* of them were fraudulent![15] That's more than you can count on one hand, pending a recount of my fingers.

---

[15] And I want to salute the 119 investigators who uncovered them.

And here's more proof, ripped straight from the headlines:[16] According to the left-leaning-due-to-the-heavy-totebag-on-their-shoulder radio network NPR, my home state of South Carolina looked into *six* allegations of voter fraud in the 2010 election and found that...

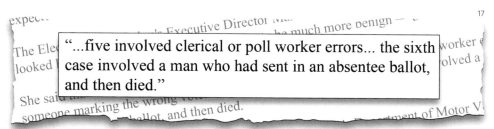

"...five involved clerical or poll worker errors... the sixth case involved a man who had sent in an absentee ballot, and then died."

You read that right, folks—voter fraud is *killing* people. And once you're dead, your name gets sent to Chicago and put on a Democratic voter roll.

And there's only one way to stop this scourge of voter fraud: End voter registration. Because the more voters, the more potential for voter fraud. Just like the more ingredients in a food, the more likely it is one of them is "Chinese drywall."

I THINK THE WHITE STUFF IS GYPSUM.

Luckily, since 2008, Idaho, Kansas, Wisconsin, Alabama, South Carolina, Tennessee, and Texas have all passed laws requiring a photo ID to vote. Problem solved, since no one's ever managed to fake a photo ID. I have that on good

---

[16] For anyone reading this after 2015, "headlines" were words written at the tops of "newspapers," which were like long tweets printed on the ground-up pulp of objects known as "trees."

[17] Source: Fessler, Pam. "In South Carolina, Dead-Voter Fraud Doesn't Quite Live Up To Fears," *NPR.org*, February 7, 2012.

authority from my personal security consultant, 47-year-old former Navy SEAL Reggie Adultperson. I met him in a bar.

Of course, with IDs, as with Italians, there are the "right" kind, and the "wrong" kind.

In Tennessee, they figured it out. The state-issued University of Tennessee student ID: no good; but a state-issued hunting license: A-OK. Because, who are you gonna turn away—the Comp Lit major or the guy you know is packing heat?

REGINALD A. ADULTPERSON. TWO TOURS IN IRAQ,
PERSONALLY ARRESTED SADDAM,
TOTALLY HAS A GIRLFRIEND.

THE INTEGRITY OF OUR ELECTIONS: HAVING SERIOUS DOUBTFIRES

NEED MORE PROOF THAT VOTER FRAUD EXISTS? LOOK AT THESE SUSPICIOUSLY SIMILAR FACES:

Clearly this man was impersonating a woman so he could vote twice for lax border laws that would allow Scottish housemaids to steal American nannying jobs. It's a travesty Robin Williams has never been tried for this crime, despite the ample and hilarious evidence on TBS.

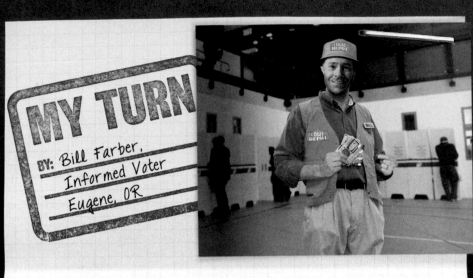

Hey, how ya doin'? Sure, I've got a minute. I'm just waiting here to vote. Then I gotta head back over to the store—pulling a triple-shift at Lowe Depot. But pretty soon I'll be on easy street—back to double-shifts. Yep. Once my guy's in charge, folks like me are gonna stop getting stomped. Hold on a sec. I'm feeling lucky about this scratch off. Palm tree... palm tree... pirate! Dammit! So close to Flamingo Badabingo!

When I get in that booth, I know exactly who I'm voting for: the guy who's gonna stop giving handouts to people like me. Haven't we gotten enough already? Because we're not getting this country back on track unless we broaden the tax base. Folks like me have no skin in the game. Or skin on the back of my wrist, after that accident with the key cutter. Point is, I'm okay paying more taxes now, when I'm pre-rich, to help future-me get the tax cuts I'll deserve.

See, I'm not one of the "haves," but I'm a have-soon. And when I'm a have-now, I want there to be more have for me to have. Speaking of which, I got an itchy scratchin' quarter ready to pay out. Ace of Diamonds... Ace of Hearts... Ace of Clubs... pirate! Crap. Almost made it to Ca$ino Ca$h $ity.

The way I look at it, raising my taxes to keep the cuts for the Job Creators isn't taking money away from me. I'm just sending my money ahead like a scout to find out what it's like to be owned by a rich guy. I'll catch up with it later. It's like those storage pods you can rent when you're moving that you put all your stuff in, and then they send it over to your new house to wait for you. Of course, my house got foreclosed, so right now, I'm living in the pod. Not bad. OK. Here we go, last scratchoff: Pyramid Scheme. Ramses... Tutankhamen... Amenhotep...pirate! Son of a bitch. I was halfway in the Mummy's Purse.

No biggie. I may be at the bottom now, but if I pay enough money up, I'll get out of this hole. It's like a grave. You get in there and start digging, and eventually, you're standing on top of the dirt pile, looking down on the sucker who just can't stop shoveling.

Woop! It's my turn to pull the lever. Wish me luck. Four years from now, when those tax cuts are mine, you'll know where to find me. I'll be living in the fanciest storage pod in town.

JUSTICE

fig 25.3-D. STEPHEN COLBERT

JURY
DUTY
SARLACC
PIT
ARBY'S
PUBLIC
BEHEADING
LETHAL
INJECTION
MARRIAGE
AM I
RIGHT?
LIFE
FRESHMAN
15
10
YEARS
5
YEARS
COMMUNITY
THEATER
COMMUNITY
SERVICE

JURY
DUTY
SARLACC
PIT
ARBY'S
PUBLIC
BEHEADING
LETHAL
INJECTION
MARRIAGE,
AM I
RIGHT?
LIFE
FRESHMAN
15
10
YEARS
5
YEARS
COMMUNITY
THEATER
COMMUNITY
SERVICE

CHAPTER SEVEN

JUSTICE

*"DR. PETERSON PROMISED ME THE LASIK
WILL BE SAFE! HE PROMISED..."*

—Lady Justice,
*on witness stand during her
malpractice lawsuit*

Since AMERICA is The Greatest Country on Earth, it naturally follows that it also has The Greatest Criminals on Earth. Sorry, China, but no one's scared of your cheap bootleg Joker, the Jorker. And to combat these Grade "A" bad eggs, we've created The Greatest Criminal Justice System on Earth as seen eight times a day on TNT in the various *Laws & Orderses*. Mind you, the police—"Order"—technically do their job before the prosecutors apply the "Law." So it should really be called "Order & Law." Show creator Dick Wolf really shanked that one. Or should I say "Wolf Dick?"

**THE JORKER
ARCHENEMY OF BANTMA**

And I have another Wolf Dick beef.[1] He leaves out the third tine of America's criminal justice spork: the brave men and women of The Greatest Corrections System on Earth. After the credits roll on *Order & Law*, these heroes safely store the convicted scumbags in the slammer, the clink, the big house, the fishtank, the

---

[1] Look for *Wolf Dick Beef* wherever issues of *Bantma* are sold.

pencil holder, the tuna salad, the lamp stand, the light switch. I could go on, but I've run out of objects in my line of sight.

That's why I was tempted to call this chapter Order & Law & Storage. And I still am!

ORDER & LAW & STORAGE

> (NOTE TO READER: WE COULDN'T AFFORD THE RIGHTS TO THE "CHUN-CHUNG" STING FROM *LAW & ORDER*, SO JUST USE THE MOST DRAMATIC SLIDE-WHISTLE YOU CAN FIND.)

ORDER

Freeze! Drop the book! Now back away slowly. Hands where I can see them.

CAN YOU STILL READ THIS WHILE BACKING AWAY? GOOD. NO SUDDEN MOVEMENTS. HEY! I SAID DON'T MOVE! THAT'S IT. TASER! TASER! TASER!

(Please rub your socks on the carpet and touch a doorknob.)

ALL RIGHT. YOU'VE BEEN SUBDUED. YOU CAN PICK UP THE BOOK NOW.

Sorry I made you ride the lightning,[2] but I had no choice. I had to prove that I know what I'm talking about when it comes to the police. And I do. A lot of my best friends are cops. We shoot the shit, and after a few drinks, we shoot shit. These guys are the real deal—regular, hardworking blue-collar folks like yours truly. Of course, my blue collar is made from chambray so I look like Jacques Cousteau.

But that's the only difference. Otherwise, me and the cops do the same work. We protect the innocent. We know when to make things look like an accident. I've even got a badge—my friend Pete passed out the night of the Policemen's Benevolent Ball. Now all I've got to do is flash it at Smoothie King, and I'm rolling in free Cranberry Cooler.

And face it. America is a festering sewer of potential criminals. I know I'd do some pretty terrible stuff if

A REGULAR JACQUES SIX-PACQUES

---

[2] I'm not sorry.

I didn't have to worry about the Fuzz.[3] We all would. Take a look in the mirror and ask yourself, "Why did I steal this mirror?" The police are the Thin Blue Line that protects you from people like you.

So, I always go out of my way to show my gratitude for the police's hard work.

THESE "NICE, WISE AMERICANS"ARE GIVING BACK.

In fact, the only folks who care about our boys in blue more than I do may be 80s rappers N.W.A., who cared so much for cops that they wrote a song about making love to them.

HOW TO TALK TO THE POLICE

If our parents raised us with love, as children we learn to live in fear of authority figures. That's why whenever you see flashing lights in your rearview mirror, you get a feeling in the pit of your stomach like you've done something wrong, or maybe one of the heroin-filled condoms you swallowed has started to leak.

But, as I said, I'm great friends with the police. They're just a big bunch of teddy bears with a rigid internal code of silence. At the end of the day they just want to get the bad guy, you know?

So as long as you're not guilty, or look like someone who might be guilty, or hesitate slightly thereby confirming your total guilt, you have nothing to worry about. Don't sweat it.[4]

Remember, all cops want is information

MAYBE HE'S COOL. *OFFER HIM A HIT.*

to solve a crime. So tell them clearly and confidently about the crime you saw, identify the black man who you think did it, and be on your way.

There will be times when you are actually guilty. When that happens and you hear the siren, don't stop. Cop cruisers don't really have the horsepower they used to. If you're good at *Grand Theft Auto*, you'll get away scot-free.

---

[3] Slang for "The Police."
[4] Sweat: also a sign of guilt.

Now, I know that some minorities claim that the police treat them "differently." That's why I've asked my friend, prominent black Republican P.K. Winsome, to give some extra tips on how to talk to the police.

{ ADDITIONAL TIPS ON TALKING TO THE POLICE } FOR PERSONS OF COLOR

BY
**P.K. WINSOME,
ENTREPRENEUR
AND
PROFESSIONAL
BLACK REPUBLICAN**

Absolutely. Thank you, Stephen. As a person of color—specifically, an African American businessman with some great deals on *Herman Cain 2012* glassware, I know that sometimes you have to go along to get along. But it's hard to go along when you're facedown in the pavement, because of the potential for fractured cheekbones. So here are some tips for my fellow AfroMotorists to ensure that we all have a safe and productive unprovoked traffic stop:

❶ Don't make any sudden moves.

❷ Don't make any gradual moves.

❸ Don't move.

❹ Keep both hands on the steering wheel of your car. (It is your car, right?)

❺ Do not carry anything that could be mistaken for a weapon, such as cell phones, wallets, combs, keys, Skittles, or hands.

❻ Do not wear the following: Hooded sweatshirts, Sweaters with hoods, Sweaters without hoods, Hoods without sweaters, Turtlenecks, Turtlehoods. Make sure all clothing is non-threatening. (examples: A. Yellow golf shirt, B. That is all.)

❼ Do not be argumentative by challenging the police with such belligerent questions as, "What did I do?" or "Why'd you pull me over?" or "Yes, officer?"

❽ When asked for your license and registration, to lighten the mood, I like to give this to the officer. You can get your own at PKjokeID.com. Order in the next 24 hours, and you will get them sooner!

❾ Be positive! Let a smile be your umbrella!

(Note: If something goes wrong and your "umbrella" ends up scattered all over the highway, check out my new website, pkdentures.com! With denture prices this low, you won't need a "bridge" loan!)

COPS LOVE THIS!

HAPPY MOTORING!

FIREPOWER

As criminals and terrorists keep enhancing their arsenals, cops find themselves playing a never-ending game of "Keeping up with whoever murdered the
Joneses." But I've got GOOD NEWS to report: police now have access to the
same weapons as our troops overseas.

THE FREEDOM TOWER

Because what's more important, America or overseas?[5]
Thanks to massive, post-9/11 Homeland Security
budgets, high-tech military hardware is showing up in
police departments everywhere—from Times Square in
New York City (pop. 8,000,000) now protected by state-
of-the-art security cameras, to Scottsbluff, Nebraska
(pop. 14,886), which is now protected by an identical
network of cameras. Sorry, Al Qaeda, but the historic
Lake Minatare Lighthouse still stands!

And Nebraska's vulnerable prairie blemishes aren't the
only weak points being fortified against our enemies.
At the time of this writing (the past), Keene, New
Hampshire (pop. 23,000) is set to receive a $286,000 Lenco BearCat armored

vehicle. This criminal-crushing freedom
monster comes complete with thermal
imaging, gun mounts, ballistic shields,
and an explosive gas detection system.
And EIGHT cup holders!

This blast-proof assault vehicle was
urgently needed because, as the city's
official request to the Department of
Homeland Security warned:

WHAT PART OF "NO SKATEBOARDING"
DO YOU KIDS NOT UNDERSTAND?

"The terrorism threat is far reaching and often unforeseen...
Keene currently hosts several large public functions to include:
an annual Pumpkin Festival..."[6]

---

[5] If you had to look down here for an answer, you're the reason cops need drones.
[6] Source: NH Department of Safety—Grants Management Unit. FY 2010 Homeland Security Grant Application.

Oh, there is nothing Mullah Omar would love more than to strike a blow against America's Pumpkin Industry.

CASE IN PROVING MY POINT:
THE 2011 NORTH DAKOTA COW CRISIS

On a hot June evening, America's drowsy summer was interrupted by news that six cows had gone missing from the Brossart family farm near the town of Rugby. So the police took appropriate action: they called in a Predator drone.

THEY HATE US FOR OUR GOURDS!

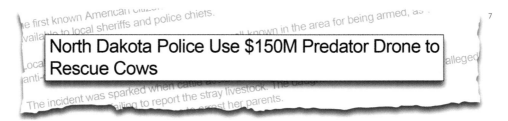

e first known American citiz...
vaila... to local sheriffs and police chiefs.
...ll known in the area for being armed, a...

North Dakota Police Use $150M Predator Drone to Rescue Cows

Loca...
anti-...
...alleged

The incident was sparked when cattle a...
...iling to report the stray livestock. The ...
...t... arrest her parents.

7

The drone's high-resolution cameras pinpointed the cow thieves and determined they were unarmed. The authorities moved in. *Think about it:* without that drone, those cows might never have been recovered. Even more troubling, we might never have eaten them.

Of course, the police can't be everywhere, that's why you must take personal responsibility for your security. For instance, I live in a gated community. The fence around my neighborhood keeps perpetrators out, unless they have access to a stool. I also have ADT Home Security. And, of course, Slomin's Home Security. I hired them to keep an eye on ADT. I mean, those ADT bastards have all my codes![8]

THESE SIGNS NOT ONLY PROTECT MY HOME, BUT SEND THE STRONG MESSAGE TO CRIMINALS THAT I HAVE DISPOSABLE INCOME AND AM PROBABLY WORTH ROBBING.

---

[7] SOURCE: *ChristianPost.com*, December 14, 2011

[8] In case I slip in the shower, and you need to get in my house, my code is 1,2,3,4,5,6—the same as my bank PIN number.

I also keep a Bible on my bedside table. This serves three functions. 1) I can swear on it to intruders that I have no valuables, 2) I can use it to remind the drug-fueled maniac with a knife to my throat of the 7th Commandment: "Thou Shall Not Steal," And 3) It's hollowed out, and I keep a gun in there.

"THE MEEK SHALL INHERIT MY LEAD!" MARK: .45

A "HI, THERE!" TO ARMS

Because, no matter how many layers of security you put between yourself and the scum, eventually the only real friend you have is a warm gun.

That's why firearms are near and dear to my heart. And thanks to my concealed carry permit, near and dear to my ankle, my right hip, either side of my ribcage, my back, and my musket balls.

In fact, firearms are the only object mentioned in the Constitution. Let that sink in, Nation. There's a reason the **Bill of Rights** doesn't cite DustBusters as being necessary to the security of a Free State—Guns are part of our **national identity**. Like Spain and bullfighting. Morocco and exotic spices. Canada and not having a national identity.

So the last thing we need is more gun regulations. Like a national gun registry. Or a 7-day waiting period. Seven whole days? By then I won't even remember why I needed a flame thrower in the first place!

WHY AM I DOING THIS AGAIN?

Isn't it restriction enough that you can buy guns only at gun shows, at gun dealers, or at Wal-Mart, or at sporting-goods stores, or at pawnshops, or from that guy your cousin knows?

Picture this: You're eating dinner with your family when suddenly four masked men burst through the window and pistol-whip you. Ask yourself: In this plausible and by no means emotionally manipulative scenario, do you really want to stand up, brush the glass off your shoulder, glare at your assailants, and say, "Leave. My. Family. *Alone!*...In seven days!"

Why would you risk that happening and permanently traumatizing your children, when you could prevent it by gunning down four men in front of them?

For all the firepower of the American Police Force, no weapon at their disposal is more effective than the **Power of Psychology**. Experienced investigators often employ a technique known as "Good Cop, Bad Cop." One friendly policeman gains the trust of a suspect by protecting him from his out-of-control partner. It's very effective.

Anyway, that's it for this part of the book. Come to think of it, where did you get this book? You paid for it, right? What's wrong? You seem a little nervous. We're just talking.

 Here's a funny story. Some people are reading this book without buying it first. You ever hear of anything like that? I'd love to hear your side of the story. Not that I'm accusing you of anything. Would you like a glass of water? Soda? Go to the kitchen. Get yourself a drink. I'll wait.

Sit down! You're lucky I don't take this book and shove it where the sun don't shine.

 Can we not do this right now?

Do what?! Discuss our personal issues at work? Am I embarrassing you in front of your precious suspect?

Hey, hey, hey, Steve! Back off.

I've got to apologize for my partner. Steve's on edge. He's on probation for use of excessive force. He collects teeth.

 A little bit, yes.

Well, excuuuuuse me.

We've wasted enough time! This creep clearly didn't buy this book. Look at those beady little eyes.

 Oh, that's mature.

You're mature!

Okay, I'm getting to it.

Look, I don't know how much longer I can control my partner so just tell me, do you know anything about this stolen book business?

Thank you.

I didn't mean it as a compliment.

Of course it is. It means I'm calm and level-headed...

You bet your ass he knows! Why do you think he's just sitting there hanging his head like that?!

...and distant and cold and cruel! That's what you are! Heartless and cruel!

He's sitting like that because he's reading.

What are you, crying?

He could be listening to this on an audiobook! You always take their side!

...Maybe.

Stephen! Steve! What the hell is going on here?!

OK. You're right. It's the captain's.

It was one time!

Oh, hey, Chief. Nothing, we're just chatting with this nice reader here.

This is all your fault! If you didn't look so guilty reading your stolen book, I wouldn't be in this mess right now.

I'm having Stephen's child!

Jesus Christ!

Hey, I want to apologize for my partner. He just heard I'm pregnant with someone else's baby. So, you really don't want him coming back in here finding out that you didn't admit to squat! He might do something ugly.

That's impossible.

Oh, is it?!

Do yourself a favor and write the worst thing you've ever done in the space provided:

Of course it is. Have you been drinking?

Is that what you think of me? That I would drink when I'm pregnant?

You're not pregnant!

_____
_____
_____
_____
_____
_____
_____
_____

Look, fellas, if you can't find a way to work it out and finish this thing, I got no choice but to put you both on suspension.

Do you hear that, reader? If you don't come clean, both of us are going to lose our jobs.

I knew it, you son of a bitch! You better get yourself a good lawyer! Or at least read the next section very carefully, scumbag. I'm gettin' too old for this shit!

And we've got a baby on the way.

No we don't.

LAW

So what happens once the police drag in the "perp?"[9] He's turned over to The Greatest Legal System in the History of the World: a system where everyone is guaranteed a speedy public trial, and many get it—where every defendant is "innocent until proven guilty." That means police can pick up a guy with blood all over his hands and the phrase "I did it!" scrawled across his forehead in his own handwriting (but backwards because he did it in a mirror), who has a DVD of the murder, with deleted scenes and special Murderer's Commentary, and we still say, "Benefit of the doubt."

This is important because all people deserve to be tried on the facts of the case.[10]

The source of these legal protections, like all things great in America, is the Constitution.[11]

THE CONSTITUTION

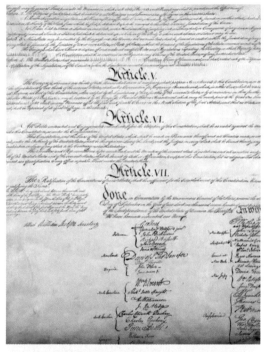

I JUST READ IT FOR THE ARTICLES

It is The Greatest Work Of Law In Human History. *We the People.* That's the first line. And yet, it gets better. *Do solemnly pursue: life and the liberty of happiness.* And I haven't even started on the treasure map on the back, which must be followed only as the Founders intended: by Nicolas Cage and a super hot blonde. It is not a "living" treasure map that activist judges can interpret to fit the whims of the day. James Madison wanted the adventurer who discovered it to turn right at the New Haven broom dasher's shoppe and canter nine furlongs as the jackdaw flies, so *that's all you're allowed to do,* even though that puts you in the westbound lane of Route 34.

---

[9] Cop slang for "perpson who did the crime."

[10] Note: Enemy combatants are not people.

[11] Corn dogs, crazy straws, the bolo tie, and Sam Elliott also have Constitutional origins.

THE AMENDMENTS

Like the Bible, the Constitution was perfect from Day One and desperately needed to be fixed. Think of the Original Articles as the Old Testament. All very nice, but where's the Jesus? Nowhere. Similarly, the original Constitution is great, but where are the guns? So they added a New Testament to the Bible, and 27 amendments to the Constitution. Naturally, just like children, some amendments turned out better than others. So for those of you who have been assigned this chapter in your Constitutional Law class, here are the Constitution's Top 27 Amendments:

THE CONSTITUTION'S TOP 27 AMENDMENTS:

1. 2nd Amendment.
2. 1st Amendment.
3. 5th Amendment: Prohibits Double Jeopardy. Someone arrest Alex Trebek.
4. 19th Amendment: Founds Suffragette City.
5. 18th Amendment: Prohibition. Leading to the creation of Bathtub Gin and Shower Schnapps.
6. 21st Amendment: Repeal of Prohibition. Which lead to the adoption of...
7. 22nd Amendment: Beer before liquor/never been sicker.
8. 6th Amendment: Guarantees a speedy trial—thanks to 24-second cross-examination clock.[12]
9. 27th Amendment: The iTunes user licensing agreement.
10. 12th Amendment: Six Trout limit.
11. 10th Amendment: Codifies calling "Shotgun!" as binding oral contract.
12. 26th Amendment: Establishes that there can be only one Highlander.
13. [13]
14. 4th Amendment: No fatties.
15. 11th Amendment: You must be *this* tall to enter BATMAN: The Ride.[14]
16. 17th Amendment: Establishes election of U.S. Senators by popular vote.

Before that, the jobs were given to the last man to keep his hand on the state's Capitol building.

17. 25th Amendment: I'm pretty sure this is the one that says America is a Christian Nation.
18. 24th Amendment: Mandates once you pop, you can't stop.
19. 20th Amendment: Presents a heartfelt *and* hilarious look back at 19 fabulous amendments.
20. 3rd Amendment: Bros before Hoes.
21. 8th Amendment: Prohibits "Cruel and Unusual Punishment" which is really a shame because we have come up with some pretty creative stuff!
22. 13th Amendment: Abolition of Slavery. Would have ranked higher, but it's kind of embarrassing that we needed it.
23. 23rd Amendment: Kismet!
24. 16th Amendment: Creates an Income Tax. But my accountant thinks he can get it down to the 12th Amendment.
25. 14th Amendment: Corporations are people.
26. 15th Amendment: Establishes the right of Habeus Porpoise, extending free squeak rights to dolphins.
27. 9th Amendment: Adds "location" to the phrase, "Location, location."

---

[12] 3-Pointer if you make your objection from behind the rail.

[13] I don't put the number 13 in my books. It's bad luck.

[14] Note: there is no height requirement for "Bantma: The Ferris Flume! How Long Can You Hold Your Breath?!"

WHEN RIGHTS GO WRONG

The greatest thing about our Constitution: its rights apply to everybody.[15] Which brings me to the worst thing about our Constitution: its rights apply to *everybody*. America is an all-you-can-eat rights buffet, and there ain't no sneeze guard, folks. Scum like convicted felons, enemy combatants, and the non-famous get their grubby germs all over the same rights *I'm* supposed to use? No, thanks. What's the point of exercising my right to a speedy trial if the witness chair gives me crabs?

Worse, these folks get out of well-deserved punishments thanks to countless

READING HIS MIRANDA RIGHTS, EVEN THOUGH
HE'S MORE OF A SAMANTHA

legal loopholes. Things like the "appeals process," "illegal search and seizure," and so-called "Miranda" rights.

This criminal coddling needs to stop—not only in real life but in our police procedural TV shows. That's valuable screen time that should be used to slowly pan over the dead stripper's body!

And felon-huggers are actively working to clog up our system with more fake rights, particularly the American Civil Liberties Union, or ACLU. And when it comes to keeping law-abiding citizens safe, they don't have A CLU.[16]

This *Union*—surprise, surprise—dedicates itself to assisting people nobody likes. For instance, the ACLU famously defended our "right to free speech"

LOGO FEATURES LADY LIBERTY TRAPPED IN A BOX WITH WATER
RISING UP TO HER CHIN. MESSAGE RECEIVED.

so that Nazis were allowed to march in the largely Jewish Skokie, Illinois. You know who else let Nazis march? The Nazis.

---

[15] Porpoises? Really? Come on!

[16] Zing! *Scorch.*

AMERICA'S JURY SYSTEM
I UNILATERALLY JUDGE IT THE FINEST IN THE WORLD

Of course, the ultimate authority in any trial is the jury, which replaces the arbitrary whims of a single judge with the arbitrary whims of 12 strangers. America's jurors are selected at random from the public to form a so-called "jury of one's peers."[17] And by peers they mean ordinary citizens who didn't come up with a good excuse to get out of jury duty—the elderly, the naïve, the unimportant-at-work. These people are truly free from bias, as well as from any plans for the next few weeks.

Sadly, some people will say just about anything to get out of jury duty, like "I'm perfect for this case. I once committed that identical stabbing!" or "I have a medical condition that requires frequent masturbation." This kind of behavior is shameful. Serving on a jury, however inconvenient, is the solemn responsibility of every American, like sitting through nine innings of baseball.

But there's an even more compelling reason to do your civic duty: It pays—as much as $40 a day for federal trials. That's like working a full shift at Taco Bell, with much less chance of coming down with Cheese Gun Wrist. In this economy, jury duty is one of the best jobs in town.

And if the money isn't incentive enough, just being surrounded by 11 average Americans is a *huge* boost to the ego. I had no idea they even made Velcro jeans.

Plus, if you're lucky enough to be picked for a high-profile case, you could even be sequestered from the public. That, my friends, is when you've hit the Big Time.

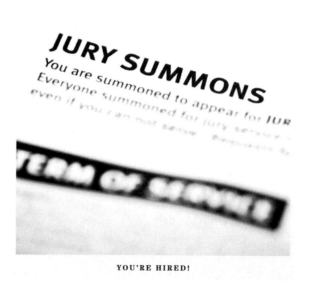

YOU'RE HIRED!

---

[17] 12 men and women. Unless you're pleading insanity, in which case it's a jury of 5 schizophrenics, six salamanders, and an angry bar of color.

For however long it takes to figure out if this guy chopped up all those toll booth operators, you'll enjoy:

★ Free accommodations at a Days Inn or equivalent sub-premium hotel outside the metropolitan center. Pro Tip: pack light to save room in your bag for free shower caps, little shampoos, and Gideon Bibles.

★ Up to $6 a day for breakfast. That's enough for an entire Denny's Grand Slam and a fistful of Sweet'N Low packets.

★ Free security-escorted rides in a windowless van.

★ Time away from your family you can credibly claim you didn't want. Now you can finally write that novel, learn to play guitar, or catch up on your bedazzling.

BEJURORED!

In other words, serving on a jury is more than just your civic duty. It's a great way to watch *Puss in Boots* for free on HBO-Latino. So, instead of trying to get out of jury duty, you should be fighting to get on—then doing everything in your power to milk that plump civic teat as long as you can. Remember, criminal cases require a unanimous verdict, meaning one self-interested contrarian can really gum up the works. For instance, I strongly believe that one self-interested contrarian can really NOT gum up the works. See how easy it is?

JUSTICE SUPERSIZED

In addition to the Best Law, America also has the **Most Law**. There are more than 1.2 million lawyers in the United States. That's almost enough to repopulate the state of New Hampshire—and then bring it to a grinding halt beneath a mountain of lawsuits.

And more lawyers are on the way! American law schools graduate over 43,000 new JDs every year. That's one every 12 minutes, which means that by the time you finish reading this chapter, you could have become a lawyer! Check your wall for diplomas!

WITH SO MUCH DEMAND FOR LAWYER ADVERTISING SPACE, OUR PARK BENCH INDUSTRY HAS RESORTED TO STACKING.

SHOULD YOU GO TO LAW SCHOOL?

If you're out of college, working an odd job, waiting for your career as a Byzantine Mosaic Tile Restorer to take off, maybe you should think about law school.

It's not a choice to be made lightly. After all, law school means three years of your life, thousands of dollars of debt, and the possibility that later on you will have to work as a lawyer.

But luckily for you, there's me! I've been around the block a few times. Ol' Stephen here knows a thing or two about the real world. So I've developed a scientific questionnaire to determine whether law school is right for you.

CAREER QUESTIONNAIRE

Hey, sit down. Do you want a drink?
__ Yes __ No

How's Denise?

_____

She seems like a great girl. Do you two ever talk about the future?
__ Yes __ No __ It's way too soon for that.

I know it *feels* too soon, but time rushes by so fast.
Seems like it was just yesterday that I taught you to ride a bike.
__ What are we talking about?

How's the bike riding going, by the way? Any problems?
__ Yes __ No

How much are you making now? $_____ . _____

That's a year?
__ Yes __ No __ Please don't start.

Do you think that's enough to raise a family on?
__ Yes __ No __ Family? I can barely take care of myself.

How is the search for_____ going?
                    (YOUR DREAM JOB: THING YOU PAINT, ACT IN, OR CROWDSOURCE)

_____

Your mother and I know how talented you are, but do you think you'll ever be as good at _____ as _____?
              (YOUR DREAM JOB: THING YOU PAINT, ACT IN, OR CROWDSOURCE)   *(JAMES FRANCO)*

__ Yes __ No

It's just that I'm sure you'll want your kids to have the same advantages we gave you.
__ Yes __ No __ I wouldn't call riding a bike an "advantage."

Did you know that before your mother became pregnant with you, I was planning to spend my life in advertising instead of marketing?
__ You've told me.

Are you getting any younger?
__ Yes __ No

Did you ever ride along with Grandpa when he was cleaning septic tanks?
__ Yes   __ No   __ Seriously, what are we talking about?

We're just talking. Can't we talk?
__ Yes   __ No

Did you know that getting a law degree doesn't mean you have to become a lawyer?
__ Yes   __ No   __ I *knew* it!

Do you think Denise wants to live like some Untouchable in Bombay?
__ Yes   __ No   __ It's Mumbai. Has been since 1996.

I suppose correcting me like that makes you feel better.
__ Yes   __ No   __ When the hell is dinner? Where's Mom?

Did you know your mother stays up nights worrying about you?
__ Yes   __ No

Did you know she had a health scare last week?
__ *What?!*

Why are you crying? _____

So you'll apply to law school?
__ Yes   __ Yes

Should we go see if dinner's ready?
__ Yes   __ No   __ Muffled sob

I hope this questionnaire helped crystallize your thinking, but remember: ultimately it's a decision only *you* can make. Good luck with the LSATs!

Stephen Colbert's Mid-Book Grin Bin!
HILARIOUS LAWYER JOKES!
(AS VETTED AND REDACTED BY BURNHAM, WHITEHEAD, BRONSTEIN AND ASSOCIATES)

DISCLAIMER: Be advised that our client, Stephen T. Colbert, has submitted a collection of his favorite lawyer jokes for publication. In limited instances, we have revised the content to ensure accuracy and minimize the potential for accusations of tortious libel. All lawyers appearing in these jokes are fictitious. Any resemblance to real lawyers, living or dead, is purely coincidental.

Dictated But Not Read
—Burnham, Whitehead,
Bronstein and Associates

EXHIBIT A

Q: WHAT DO YOU CALL 100 LAWYERS AT THE BOTTOM OF THE OCEAN?
A: A potentially lucrative wrongful death suit against the tour boat operator. Punitive damages, future wages, and loss of companionship may exceed eight figures.

Q: WHY DID THE LAWYER CROSS THE ROAD?
A: Objection. The witness is being asked to speculate as to intent.

Q: HOW MANY LAWYERS DOES IT TAKE TO CHANGE A LIGHTBULB?
A: Electrical work should be performed only by a licensed electrician in full compliance with all local and Federal construction codes. If said electrician is additionally an attorney duly qualified and admitted to practice in the jurisdiction of the bulb changing, then under normal circumstances, a single lawyer is generally sufficient. The lightbulb, however, is urged to retain counsel.

& STORAGE

You've probably heard a lot of talk about a "housing crisis" from America's Negative Nellies. Well, nice try, Nellies. And notice, I'm not calling you "Nice-Try Nellies," who, unlike their negative brethren, are at least making an effort.

Besides, how can there be a housing crisis when 2.3 million Americans live in homes that *don't cost them a penny*? Those folks are the fortunate residents of the Greatest Prison System on Earth.

Like everything America does, we do prison BIG. Here's one of my patented **stats**: 1 out of every 135 Americans is currently incarcerated. So look around the Waffle House where you're reading this: at least one person in the restaurant is an escaped prisoner who has fled to somewhere with familiar food.

When it comes to processing citizens into inmates, no other nation on earth can touch America. And if they

ULTIMATE GATED COMMUNITY

do touch America, that's a minimum 5-10 (or Life, if they have a joint in their pocket.) Because prisoner-creation is the only manufacturing sector where we beat China. With a fourth of China's population, we have nearly *twice* their prisoners. Who's better at math, now?

If you include inmates, parolees, and folks on probation, there are more people in American jails than ever labored in Stalin's Gulags or Mao's reeducation camps. Looks like we win the Cold War again, Commies!

TIP OF MY HAT—OR TASSELED FEZ, OR WHATEVER THEY WEAR OVER THERE

One thing I will give the Chinese props for is they have us beat when it comes to plastinating their ex-cons as display corpses for the *Bodies* exhibit.

Nothing in the entire U.S. Judicial System can reach the level of this actual disclaimer by Premier, the producers of the *Bodies* exhibit:

> *This exhibit displays human remains of Chinese citizens or residents which were originally received by the Chinese Bureau of Police. The Chinese Bureau of Police may receive bodies from Chinese prisons. Premier cannot independently verify that the human remains you are viewing are not those of persons who were incarcerated in Chinese prisons.*

> *With respect to the human parts, organs, fetuses and embryos you are viewing, Premier relies solely on the representations of its Chinese partners and cannot independently verify that they do not belong to persons executed while incarcerated in Chinese prisons.*

Still want to shoplift that cell phone, Ju-Long? Because the Chinese police may or may not plastinate you for the amusement of the "round eyes." But it doesn't even matter if they actually do it. The true deterrence is just the *possibility* that your exposed vascular system might spend eternity playing volleyball in the lobby of the Luxor in Vegas.

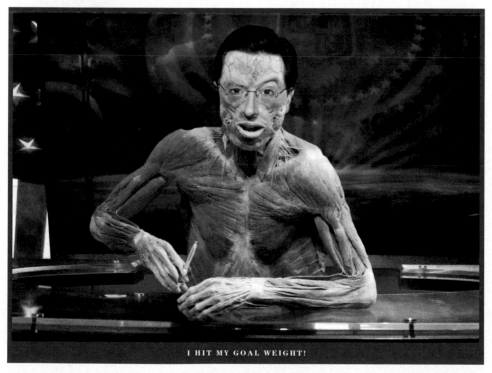

I HIT MY GOAL WEIGHT!

PRIVATE PRISONS:
WHERE THE FREE MARKET CAPTURES ITS PREY

One reason we have the best prison system in the world is because we have turned a lot of it over to the private sector.

Private prisons are the greatest jail innovation since affixing Jell-O mounds to a cafeteria tray and smuggling it back to your cell to mimic a woman's embrace.

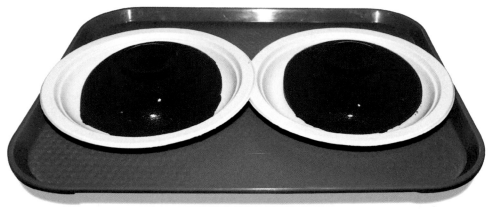

TREAT HER LIKE A LADY

Thanks to the free market, private prisons have more incentive to keep the public safe. Government prisons stay open even if they're empty, just like national parks and Detroit. But private prisons are paid per inmate; the higher their populations, the more money they make. And since their profits go up with each new inmate, private prisons have an incentive to protect the public by locking up criminals, potential criminals, and anyone who ever ended up as the murderer in a game of Clue.

And private prisons use those profits to promote even higher occupancy, by lobbying lawmakers to pass harsher laws. These lead to more inmates, and more inmates lead to more profits, which in turn lead to more harsh laws. It's the Circle of Life Imprisonment!

Looking at the numbers, odds are at least a third of you reading this book have checked it out of the prison library. That's why I instructed my publisher to make the cover out of a pliant board stock impregnated with epoxy that can easily be formed into a shiv when soaked in toilet water. You're welcome, gentlemen. Just remember what I did for you if we ever meet in the low-security yard.

HOW TO FASHION MY BOOK INTO A SHIV

fig. 1 CHECK OUT BOOK FROM LIBRARY.
MOVE UP PIRATE SHIP ON YOUR
READING ADVENTURE WALL MAP!

fig. 2 TEAR OFF FRONT COVER. DO NOT
DAMAGE IMAGE OF MY FACE.

fig. 3 SOAK IN TOILET WATER. THEN PUT
THE SEAT DOWN FOR THE LADIES.
YOU LIVE IN JAIL, NOT A BARN.

fig. 4 ROLL INTO TUBE.

fig. 5 SHARPEN.

fig. 6 STAB LITTLE MIKE.

And to my few non-con readers, let me be the first to say, they will eventually catch you doing that thing that you thought you could get away with, and you'll be heading to the penitentiary. Well, lucky for you, I've spent years plotting exactly how I'd survive in prison, get the better of the system, then ultimately break out with Steve McQueen.

YOU'VE GOT JAIL!

TIPS FOR SERVING A LIFE SENTENCE ... OF FUN!

Surviving the big house takes cunning, animal instincts, and a body covered in graphic White-Power tattoos. Follow my tips and before you can say "Shawshank Redemption," you'll rise through the ranks of the inmate population and wind up winning your freedom.

★ Learn prison slang. "Ink" means "tattoos," "Paper" is code for "package of drugs," "fish" is a "newcomer," "fission" means "splitting nuclei," while "fusion" means "creating heavier ones," and "Gimme them triangles" means "Pass the toast points." (White-collar prison only.)

★ Make a name for yourself in the prison yard. When all the other meatheads are grabbing the free weights, grab the oft-overlooked rhythmic gymnastic ribbon and put on a show that will rock everyone to their emotional core.

★ Control the flow of drugs in prison. Mastermind a muling system whereby your conjugal visitors swallow copious amounts of Oxy before arrival, then vomit them into the boom-boom trailer's restroom toilet. Once you're stocked up, find the spoon-dug crawlspace under the bench-press machine, emerge in C-block, look for the guard with the eyepatch, and ask for D-Nasty.

★ Get a useful prison job: In the metal shop, you can grind a license plate down into a deadly throwing blade that also honors your home state of New Hampshire.

★ Wear one of those prison hairnet kinda things. This not only says, "I'm a badass," but also, "I care about safe food preparation."

★ If MSNBC's *Lockup Raw* comes to your facility, ham it up and make a name for yourself. We all remember such beloved characters as "tossed salad guy,"[18]

---

[18] What was his name again?

but there's still room for a "That neo-Nazi who crochets" or "That embezzler with the Samurai topknot."

★ Learn the harmonica. There's no better way to musically capture the sadness and loneliness of prison. Except, of course, a tenor sax, but good luck fitting that in your rectum.

★ For your own safety, avoid the major gangs: the Aryan Brotherhood, the Crips, the Bloods, the Latin Kings— they've cornered their demos. Carve out your own niche: I'd go with "the Zionist Conspiracy," a group of yard-hardened Hasids whose fearsome reprisals are matched only by the fury of their klezmer dancing.

★ Whatever you do, don't ever drop the soap in the shower! You don't want to get a reputation as clumsy. Lifelong incarceration hurts, but not as much as being picked last for the prison softball team.

"*SHALOM*, NEW MEAT.
TOSS MY KREPLACH."

CLOSING ARGUMENT

But remember, even though you are guilty as sin, you don't have to go to jail. All you need is a lawyer who believes in you. And who believes in you more than you? I don't.

Well, you're in luck because our legal system will let you defend yourself in court. And as I have learned from movies and television, the outcome of any case hinges solely on a moving and dramatic closing argument.

So I have prepared for you the mother of all closing arguments. Feel free to spend the trial sexting ex-girlfriends, because you're guaranteed a win when you stand up, take a slow drink of water, adjust your suspenders, and unload this baby…

BRAMLETT ABERCROMBIE
SIMPLE COUNTRY LAWYER FOR THE DEFENSE

Ladies and gentlemen of the jury, your honor, the bailiff, the stenographer, fine citizens in the gallery, members of the Academy: You've heard many arguments against me over the past several weeks. You've heard the prosecution's so-called "mountain of circumstantial, eye-witness, forensic, and video evidence."

All have been presented to you in the cynical confidence that their version of events would not be doubted; confident that you, the jury, would go along with them on the assumption—the evil assumption—that all accused men lie; are basically immoral; are not to be trusted around our women. Well, I am to be trusted around your women. I can prove it! Bring me your women!

But where are your women? Today, I stand here alone. And you call this justice. Just ask yourself: (Point to self) Is this the face of a [insert crime here]? The answer is clearly no. Look, I'm smiling!

Could a guilty person be this carefree?

Also ask yourself, if this crime did indeed happen, was it committed against you? No. Does it affect you? No. Then what business is it of yours? I don't come into your homes and judge you. And by the looks of you, I'm pretty sure some of you have done some unspeakable, heinous acts that would give a carny nightmares. The fact is, this case should never even have come to trial. Did you see me commit the crime? Well then, I submit, that the security camera footage of me committing it amounts to nothing more than hearsay.

Ladies and Gentlemen, *(gently pat sweat off your brow with a crisp handkerchief)* even though I stand accused of terrible crimes, I want you to do something. I want you to close your eyes. Go on, close them. Envision these shameful acts as they were being committed. Can you see it? Do you have a mental picture in your head? Good. Now imagine that they are being committed by *someone other than me*. Do you see him? He doesn't even look like me. The hair is totally off! This trial is a sham! Why are we even here?! *(pick up a mug and throw it at the prosecutor.)*

Look! He caught it with his right hand! There's your man!

In summation: I object. Overruled! I'll allow it. I'm out of order? If it please the court, you're out of order. The whole damn system is out of order! And the bathroom's out of toilet paper. You can't handle the truth! Are you talkin' to me? Twelve angry men! Angry? I'm mad as hell and I'm not going to take it anymore! If there's something strange in your neighborhood, who you gonna call? My cousin Vinnie.

I rest my case. Take your time deliberating. I'll hang up and listen for my answer off the air.
(Triumphantly walk out of the courtroom at a brisk clip.)

FOOD

fig 26.3-D. **STEPHEN COLBERT**

CHAPTER EIGHT

FOOD

"EAT IT. JUST EAT IT."
—Alfred M. Yankovic,
Poet Laureate of the United States

Merriam-Webster defines the word "Food" as "*n. Any nourishing substance that is...*" I didn't read the rest.

I got hungry from all that reading, tossed the dictionary aside and ate a burrito off my chest while watching *Storage Wars.* Then I got hungry from all that TV and ate a sleeve of Ritz crackers, followed by a pant leg of Oreos, and a windbreaker of Crunch 'n Munch.

ASK FOR THE "ENDANGERED KHAKIS"

Now, it goes without saying that American Food is the best—from American cheese to American Eagle Outfitters, the foremost purveyor of black market eagle meat.

As we all know, you are what you eat. And I'm proud to say Americans are the tastiest, crispiest, saltiest, most thoroughly processed corn-based people on Earth. Plus, we come in enormous portions, and our packaging is bright and cheery.

When you think of American food, you think of *abundance.* We have so much food in this country that in 1867 we had to buy Alaska just for the freezer space.

CONTENTS MAY SETTLE OVER TIME

PRESENTLY DEFROSTING

"Chew" on this fact:[1] No famine has ever occurred in a functioning democracy. And since America is the best democracy in History, we naturally have the most food. So the next time your significant other says you're getting a little paunchy, you tell them that you're not fat, **you're just extra free.**

American food boasts something no other country can offer: the sweet taste of man's triumph over nature. If you can plant it, grow it, or graze it, Americans can formulate it in a test tube using common household products, and do so minus the distracting nutrients.

But the main thing America's done to food is to produce tons and tons of it. We're a top exporter of beef, grain, fruits, vegetables, poultry, as well as foods that fall into no known category, like Tyson's Any'tizers Chicken Fries.

ARE THEY CHICKEN? ARE THEY FRIES? THE ANSWER IS "ANY."

THE CORN IDENTITY: CORN IN AMERICA

We produce so much food we can pour the leftovers into our cars, in the form of corn-based ethanol. Thanks to generous farm subsidies that keep the price of corn low, American businesses have been able to process corn into absolutely anything and everything: snack foods, drinks, eggs, cereal, animal feed—even the all-American hot dog is 96% corn and 4% corn anus.

"I DRINK YOUR
HIGH-FRUCTOSE CORN SYRUP!"

Corn's in our pesticides, wallpaper, plaster-boards, joint compounds, cardboard boxes, cosmetics, batteries, and vitamins. It's even in our footnotes.[2]

Corn is so versatile, it's the Daniel Day Lewis of American staple crops.

With all this corn being crammed into our corn holes, it should come as no surprise that we are mostly corn. Want proof? Corn has ears. We have ears. Coincidence? Or Corn-cidence?!

---

[1] This has an hilarious double meaning.
[2] Corn!

★ ★ ★

Of course, Americans don't just grow food, we *change* it. We make it saltier and fattier, which is to say, American-er. (After all, freedom isn't sugar-free.) In 1974, we made history by being the first nation to put pizza on a bagel. To date, Russia's snack program has barely mustered the technology to put a monkey on a latke.

SO CLOSE.

Then we learned how to stuff foods inside other foods to create whole new foods, like turducken (a chicken inside of a duck inside of a turkey) or Oreyohos (an Oreo inside of a Yodel inside of a Ho Ho).[3]

IT'Z DELICIOUZ![5]

Plus, we can make food look like other food. Take the McRib Sandwich, which is shaped like ribs but is mostly pork shoulder and mortician's putty. Or Wyngz, which look like chicken wings, but come from chyckynz.[4]

And thanks to Monsanto's genetically engineered seeds, we will soon be able to grow potatoes that can take the SATs for you.

Sure, there's a chance that somewhere in our fiddling, we switch on the gene for fruit-onset Parkinson's. But as the saying goes, you can't make a sentient fruit salad without breaking a few watermelons that now hatch from eggs.

As everyone knows, when left in its natural state, food is disgusting. Take the pomegranate, a horrifying alien womb of a fruit filled with tiny juice pupae. But that's only one of nature's disgusting edible pranks. Why are there artichokes? They look like something they shoved up a heretic's rectum during the Spanish Inquisition. Sure, artichoke leaves taste good dipped in a buttery Hollandaise. But so do Huggies.

REALLY HOLDS THE SAUCE

---

[3] Add frozen yogurt to make Froyoreyohos.
[4] Which hatch from egz.
[5] My compliments to the chemist!

JUST LOOK AT SOME OF THE FOODS WE'VE BEEN ABLE TO IMPROVE UPON!

FOOD	IMPERFECT NATURAL STATE	IMPROVEMENT	BONUS
TOMATOES	They don't all ripen at the same time; some aren't perfectly round.	We gas them with ethylene to make them red and breed them to be uniform size, and so tough they make the crisper their bitch.	Our tomatoes are now subject to respiratory illness because their tongues are too big for their mouths. Also, they have tongues and mouths.
MILK	There are minutes, if not hours, of every day that our dairy cows are not producing it.	Thanks to recombinant bovine growth hormone, our cows are producing twice as much milk as before!	So are our 8-year-old girls!
POTATOES	They are vulnerable to the potato beetle. How did they not see that coming?	We made them beetle-resistant with genetic modifying, and also by spraying them with an "entomopathogenic fungus."	Their eyes now follow me around the room.
SUGARCANE	Too much cane, not enough sugar.	We gave it an even higher sucrose content— approaching the level found in most Americans.	It has been trained to harvest itself when it hears the command, "Gimme some sugar."
HONEY	Honey didn't really need to be improved, although those squeeze bottles shaped like bears scare me.	Since some bees collect nectar from genetically modified canola plants, we get genetically modified honey we didn't intentionally create. Who knows in what ways it's better? Exciting!	Honey Nut Cheerios are now a male contraceptive.

THE FRANKENFLAVORFICATION OF
THE AMERICAN BLANDSCAPE

For the record, I believe America's food scientists are national heroes. They are second only to NASA's engineers in their efforts to propel man to the limits of his natural environment. But for every conveniently stackable square chicken, an abomination slips through the R&D department.

When I was but a lad, you had only four (4) types of gum: Wrigley's Spearmint, Juicy Fruit, Bazooka Joe, and those carpenter shims that came with baseball cards.

But these days, chewing gum is as supple and flamboyant as a Saigon Ladyboy. Case in point, Stride *"Shift"* Flavor-Changing Gum.

CHUPAUL?

You heard me: "Flavor-Changing." The gum starts out as one flavor, then blindsides the taste buds with a different and sometimes unwelcome flavor! What once was Berry is now inexplicably Mint. God's natural order has been upturned right inside the temple of your own mouth! It should be obvious to all that Stride is nothing more than a bi-curious gum threatening to destroy the sanctity of straight flavorage. Is it exciting? Sure! Illicit? Yes. But I believe being minty is a choice.

Stride has to get their act together, and do the right thing: suppress its burning desire to swing, accept Jesus, and settle down into a flavorless marriage with a pack of sugar-free Trident.

GO AHEAD AND CHEW, BUT NO TONGUE!

GUN TO MY HEAD:
WHICH AMERICANS I WOULD EAT AND WHY

It may make some uncomfortable, but any truly complete discussion of food must take us to the very outer limits of cuisine: cannibalism. The prospect of eating human flesh is horrific to contemplate, especially since cannibalism is done in only the most desperate situations, frequently without proper utensils or seasonings. But these are desperate times, making it surprisingly easy for me to come up with multiple scenarios in which I would eat people. So, here's a list of folks I would consume if we were caught in a terrible life-or-death, no-way-out scenario, as well as some tips for side dishes and wine pairings.

MATTHEW MCCONAUGHEY

GRASS FED

This popular actor has been selling himself as a fine cut of man-meat for years. Take any McConaughey torso from any glossy celebrity magazine beach-body pictorial, and it would look perfectly at home on a little Styrofoam tray, cling wrapped, date-stamped and placed in your grocers' display case next to the smoked Clooney.

I usually like my cuts well-marbled, but I have no doubt that Matt would be delicious. This isn't weird because Matt's a friend. For McConaughey, I think I'd keep it simple. Perhaps a balsamic vinegar reduction paired with a nice light Pinot. Again, I would only do this if Mr. McConaughey and I were the last two survivors of a sunken cruise ship, he was near death, and I found some balsamic vinegar and a bottle of Pinot. (This is highly unlikely to ever happen, Matt. Please respond to my invitations to join me on a midwinter cruise.)

My only concern is that the THC levels in the prominent stoner's body would give me a contact high. Let's face it—during the consumption of human flesh is no time to become paranoid.

SENATOR JOE LIEBERMAN

Would Joe Liebermeat be Kosher? That's a question for the Sage Rabbis of Old, but I doubt any of them would be available for a consultation in the collapsed mine shaft Joe and I would have to be in for me to even contemplate a tiny nosh of the Senator from Connecticut. That said, I'd first go for the jowl meat, which looks moist, tender, and milk-fed enough to work in any veal recipe. And since it could take the rescue drillers weeks to dig me out, there'll be more than enough time to slow-cook my Joe Osso Bucco until the meat is just falling off his cheekbones (which I assume are in there, somewhere).

**I BE-LIEB
I CAN FRY**

STEVEN TYLER

If I were on Aerosmith's tour bus when it careened off a mountain cliff, and the other band members had to walk through the desert to the nearest town for help, I think Mr. Tyler would be the perfect backup food source. Who knows how long it would take rescue crews to arrive, if ever, but there would be no need to refrigerate Steve Meat even in the harshest conditions, as he comes pre-jerkied.

**DUDE (LOOKS LIKE
AN ENTRÉE)**

RACHAEL RAY

I'm not sure under what circumstances Rachael Ray and I would be stranded together in eat-or-be-eaten desperation, so for simplicity's sake, let's say a meteor will be hitting the Earth within the hour. The advantages of eating Ms. Ray should be apparent: *she can give me the perfect recipe to make her into a 30-minute meal!*

**YUM-O! I MEAN,
I HAD
NO CHOICE.**

STEPHEN COLBERT

Having accidentally bitten the inside of my cheek on a few occasions, I know I am delicious.

**BEST PART IS, I WOULDN'T
GAIN A POUND.**

TV DINNER

No other country is as food-obsessed as America. Our national pastime, besides home-blood-sugar testing, is watching food on television. And our fixin's-fetish is all thanks to the brave pioneers of televised cooking: James Beard, The Frugal Gourmet, and Julia Child.

HEY, STREEP! PLAY THE CHICKEN NEXT TIME, AND I'LL BE IMPRESSED.

But now you've got Food Network, The Cooking Channel, and, of course, Animal Planet, because in America, we don't settle for constantly eating food with our mouths, we also demand to chew it with our eyes. That's why our TVs are brimming with so much hot man-on-pan action. You can't channel surf for long without seeing a turkey getting stuffed over and over until they finally cut to the gravy shot. And like you, I can't get enough. I started watching food at a young age. In fact, I still keep an old stack of *Gourmet* magazines from the 70s under my mattress—back before they waxed away their thatches of angel hair pasta.[6]

And the current onslaught of food-nography isn't limited to dedicated food channels. There's Bravo: *Top Chef, Top Chef Just Desserts, Top Chef Masters, Chef Roblé and Co., Around the World in 80 Plates, Rocco's Dinner Party.* Bravo has so many cooking shows that I can only conclude that gays must eat food.

I had no idea, based on informal polls of their body fat. I always assumed they subsisted solely on the excitement of renovating a brownstone.

Even major networks are tweaking their hit shows to attract foodies, which explains why each Sunday *60 Minutes* has stories reported by a dried yam.

Indeed, America now has enough food-based programming to fill 24 hours of television, seven days a week. To put that in perspective, deep-fry your TV and eat it.

"SWEET POTATO" SAFER

---

[6] And all the melons were real!

TYPICAL LATE-NIGHT TELEVISION SCHEDULE:

☐ Tonight's Highlights   **PRIME TIME Saturday 5/12**

Channel	7 p.m.	8 p.m.	9 p.m.	10 p.m.
food network	Cover it with Cheese!	Put It In Your Mouth!	Mo', Please! with Mo Rocca	The Deadliest Ketchup
COOKING CHANNEL	Roast Rage	Nigella Lawson Sticks Her Finger in Soft Things	Morbidly Gourmet	Swamp Chefs
HISTORY	Flight of the Luftwaffle	Blintz-krieg	Nazi Cornbread Recipes	Inside Hitler's Spice Rack
C-SPAN	Water About To Boil	Mitch McConnell Reads His Gravy Recipe Into the Congressional Record	Toaster Watch 2012	Rep. Buck McKeon On How He Could Really Go For Some Thai
TCM TURNER CLASSIC MOVIES	Meat John Dough	What Ever Happened to Baby Carrots?	When Harry Met Salad	Mr. Smith Goes to White Castle

And the reason these shows are selling like hotcakes[7] is because America is in the midst of a true renaissance of food you can't taste. Take Guy Fieri—so committed to consumption that he uses ranch dressing as hair gel and refuses to wipe off what appears to be zesty wing sauce that's collected around his mouth.

But the greatest thing about today's food renaissance is that you no longer need to be a chef to be on TV. The only prerequisite to food stardom is knowing what hole to jam it in.

SOMEONE GET THIS GUY A WET-NAP

---

[7] *Selling Like Hotcakes* on Tuesdays at 4 p.m. on Food Network.

MAN V. FOOD: FOOD IS YOUR FRIENEMY

In *Man v. Food*, host Adam Richman travels from city to city across America doing what most Americans can only dream of: hitting a few landmarks, then being cheered on by locals while attempting to eat a seven-pound burrito.

You see, America is the only country on Earth with so much food that its people have an adversarial relationship with sustenance. Food is coming at us from all directions. How many times have you been minding your own business, then suddenly found yourself

RICHMAN KNOWS THAT TO STAY ON TOP OF THE FOOD CHAIN, YOU MUST EAT THE FOOD, CHAIN AND ALL.

surrounded by empty Arby's wrappers and filled with a vague sense of having been violated?

Our anger at food is the envy of the world. So the next time you don't want to finish that Wendy's Double Baconator,[8] just remember there's a starving kid in Africa who would love to hate himself for eating it.

ENTER THE FOOD POLICE

There's a chorus of naysayers out there who have made it their business to keep America stuck in the past. I'm talking about the Foodstapo like Eric Schlosser, Michael Pollan, and Alice Waters, who want us to grow our own food in community gardens and on rooftops. Sorry, but last time I tried it, my ceiling couldn't handle the weight of a John Deere tractor. Canopy bed saved my life.

These self-described "locavores"[9] are trying to squash agri-business by encouraging us to "eat locally." Sorry, but I want to eat a chicken that's seen the world, not some provincial loser capon who's free-ranging it at a poultry commune. I want a chicken with some miles on it. I want to taste the petroleum from the cargo hold, where it was flash frozen on an unregulated Indonesian barge. And should it give me a food-borne illness, who cares? Those 10 pounds I drop from vomiting will just help me fit back into my old high school jeans. It's a win-win.

I'M JUST ONE BAD CLAM AWAY, OLD FRIEND.

---

[8] It "Bacons" at you.
[9] Latin for "eaters of crazy."

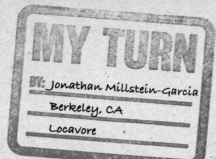

MY TURN

BY: Jonathan Millstein-Garcia

Berkeley, CA

Locavore

Greetings and namaste. If you're reading this letter, it means that Treefrog, my bicycle messenger, made it to New York. (I swore off the Postal Service after they ignored my petition to convert their fleet to recumbent bicycles.) Kindly offer Treefrog a cup of green tea before sending him back to Berkeley, won't you?

The purpose of my letter is simple: to forever change the world's approach to food production and transport, and to get credit for it. If I should fail, there will be nothing left to slow us from our suicidal course with the irreversible destruction of our ecosystem. And my only solace will be that it was all your fault.

You see, there was a time in America when we knew where our food came from. It came from no farther than a farmer could steer his ox cart, which is why our diet consisted largely of hardtack and turnips splattered with ox dung. Local ox dung. These days, our tables spilleth over with chiles from Turkey, turkeys from Chile, Swedish fish from Switzerland, and Swiss Miss from Wisconsin. The only thing American about the average American meal it is how much fossil fuel it burned getting to us.

Well, not in the Millstein-Garcia household. I always know precisely where my food comes from, as well as where my food's food came from, and where my food's food's food came from. I draw the line at 10 food generations, which is regrettably unambitious but still six generations further than I can trace my family. Unfortunately, Great-Great-Grandma Beatrice was not certified organic.

I wish that you could be here with me to witness the locally grown bounty that is springtime in Northern California. The Victoria rhubarb have just come into season, their pink stalks blushing like a young girl at her first lute recital. I picked up a fresh bunch at the farmer's market this morning for a mere $18. I must find a use for them before this evening, when they go back out of season.

Lars, my local source for poultry (except ducklings, which I raise myself in the upstairs bathtub), stopped by earlier today with fresh eggs. I insist on only the freshest ingredients, which means that Lars holds each hen so they can lay directly into my mixing bowl. The occasional tail feather in my béarnaise is well worth the rich, silky sense of superiority. Things can get a little tricky when I'm making custard, as I have limited counter space to perch a Holstein cow. I must discuss that with the artisanal cabinet maker building my new kitchen set using only colonial-era tools. Every re-design sets him back 12 years.

Tomorrow I'll take the unicycle up to visit Lord Byron, the Tamworth hog being raised by a local Comp Lit professor for our winter sausage. Unlike factory farm pigs, which are confined to cramped enclosures, Lord Byron has the run of a five-acre estate, complete with a spring-fed wallowing hole, ropes course, and archery range. In the evenings, there's live chamber music. The humane treatment is clearly paying off, as Lord Byron has already acquired a fifth-grade reading level. We haven't yet decided, but we'll prob-ably use a blend of alder and cherry wood to smoke his back fat. Of course, Lord Byron will be asked to weigh in.

As you can see, eating a strictly local diet is both practical and economical, particularly if you are independently wealthy and have unlimited free time. And to the shrill critics who cry that most Americans have enough trouble getting sufficient food on the table without worrying about where it came from, I say: Please keep it down; you're upsetting my heirloom zucchinis. They just came off their antidepressants.

FOREIGN FOODS:
INTERNATIONAL INCIDENTS DU JOUR

Being a nation of immigrants, we're all the more grateful because we remember the foods we escaped in our various Old Countries:

Russian Borscht

What happens to Russian beets when they lose all hope and drown themselves.[10]

Scottish Haggis

Imagine the disembowelment scene in *Braveheart*, but as a main course.

German Blutwurst, or "blood sausage"

The second worst thing the Germans have ever done.

Sardinian Casu Marzu

Rotten cheese filled with maggots that when disturbed, leap into your face. Contains 100% of the Recommended Daily Allowance of leaping maggots.

When we got to America, we cast off all those oppressive dishes and began making foods that reflected our diversity. Our food was all about choice: 31 flavors. 57 varieties. 99 problems, but a Manwich™ ain't one.

And our culinary freedom is as unlimited as our breadsticks. America is the land of opportunity. Where else could a lowly Transylvanian immigrant who arrived here with nothing but a dream and the cape on his back become America's premier pitchman of dessert-based breakfast cereal.

ORIGINAL NAME: CHAIM CHOCOLAWICZ

---

[10] Tragic Stewicide.

FOREIGN CUISINE

But food is more than just an energy source, national pastime, intoxicating lover, trusted confidant, and designated emergency contact.

Food is as American as apple pie. And I'd shout that from sea to shining sea, if it weren't for all the pie in my mouth. America eats every other country under the table. Then we eat the table—a great source of fiber!

That's why it's so important that we pay attention to the many foreign foods encroaching on American sovereign stomachs: Mexican, Chinese, French, and Italian. If I had the time, I could name literally thousands of other countries.[11]

Sorry, but the easily identifiable, under-processed junk other countries call food just doesn't pass mustard for me. Worst of all, when I ask for mustard to be passed, Japanese waiters act like I'm crazy. But I'm prepared to defend American food until my dying breath, which given my Slim Jim intake, could be Thursday.

So to help you stay vigilant, I've put together this guide for pragmatic cuisine-ophobes out there. Eat 'em and weep:

DR. KER-PORK-IAN

CHINESE FOOD

BIG TROUBLE IN LITTLE INTESTINE

Honestly, I can't tell you which Chinese dish I dislike the most: the #41 or the #16. To me, it all tastes like a steaming pile of #2.[12] General Tso should be tried for War Crimes against my colon. I've got the grim pictures to prove it, but for some reason The Hague keeps sending them back.

But the final insult comes with their so-called "desserts." Like the "fortune cookie,"[13] the only dessert so boring it comes with reading material.[14]

---

[11] Off the top of my head: Brazil... and others.

[12] #2 is The Three Kingdom Tofu Noodles. Tastes like shit.

[13] Or as I call it, the fortune MIS-cookie!

[14] In bed!

MEXICAN FOOD

Mexican, or "Latina," food is undeniably growing in popularity, even seen from a purely condiment-based perspective. Salsa now accounts for more sales by volume than the annual totals racked up by ketchup, catsup, and fancy ketchup combined. Am I alarmed? ¡Alarmed enough to use a hysterical upside-down Mex-clamation[15] point at the beginning of this sentence!

BURRITOS: THE BODY-BAG OF FOOD

Yes, I've heard all the hype about Mexican food. It's "spicy" and "exciting" and even "microwaveable." But I've also heard things like, "Did I just eat dirt?" It may not win me any so-called "Amigos" to say so, but let's face facts: Every Mexican meal comes with significant risk of digestive distress. We've all been there.[16]

There is one Mexican item that I do enjoy: their ingenious Taco Salad. It's everything you find in every other Mexican dish—corn tortilla, meat, beans, onion, avocado, soap—but in a bowl you can **eat**! They never need to wash a dish![17]

I CONQUIST-*ADORE* THIS!

SPANISH TAPAS

My least favorite kind of Mexican food. These tiny plates were originally made to be set on top of sangria glasses to protect their precious fruit booze from flies. Great idea! "Flies in my wine? Horrible![18] Flies in my food? Fantastico! Now let us all make love[19] and take a four hour nap."

And as much as I love how these tiny plates make

WAITER, THERE'S A FLY IN MY EVERYTHING!

---

[15] ¡Copyright! Stephen Colbert, 2012.

[16] Toilet.

[17] Then again, I never have to wash a dish, either. I have that special kind of sink where you just dump your dirty dishes into it, and when you come back later they've been rinsed off and put in the dishwasher. I also have that special kind of dishwasher that puts the clean dishes back in the cupboards for you while you're at work or after you've gone up to bed. My wife loves it—sometimes she stays down in the kitchen after I've gone up to bed, I assume to watch it work.

[18] Though it would pair nicely with the maggots in my cheese.

[19] Thanks a lot, Spanish flies!

me feel like a Giant rampaging through a village of grilled octopus, they also promote sharing. And folks, that's gastro-socialism! In fact, if you rearrange the letters in TAPAS, and then replace a few of them with different letters, you end up with CASTRO!

ETHIOPIAN FOOD

GOOD LORD! WHAT HAVE YOU BEEN EATING?

I'd love to crap on Ethiopian food, but by the looks of it, someone beat me to it.

Plus, it's just cruel to gorge on Ethiopian food when so many Ethiopians are starving. That's why no matter what exotic spices they pour into their dishes, to me, all Ethiopian food tastes like guilt. So whenever I go to Queen of Sheba, I get a to-go bag, take it to Fed Ex, and send it to Bono. So far, not one thank-you note!

MIDDLE EASTERN FOOD

Nation, it's no secret, I don't trust Middle Eastern food. That's right—I've got the deep-fried falafel balls to finally say it. I have good reason to be suspicious. For starters, almost every dish seems to be made from chickpeas, better known by its Nom de Legume: Garbanzo Beans. What are these chickpeas trying to hide? I say we toss these chickpeas into Gitmo, possibly with some garlic, olive oil and lemon juice.

OSAMA BEAN LADEN

FRENCH FOOD

LE FOOD

The NPR crowd may love their "complex sauces" that "titillate the palate" and "seduce the senses." But when I'm eating, the last thing I want to worry about is a piece of chicken trying to get to third base with my tongue.

SCANDINAVIAN FOOD

Here's a list of things that use lye as an ingredient: biodiesel, oven cleaner, meth, and the traditional Norwegian dish lutefisk. Given the choice, I'd rather eat the first three.

But I will give these Norse trolls credit for one thing: the Smörgåsbord. I hope I'm spelling that right. I just slammed my hands on the keyboard a few times and that's what came up. Smörgåsbording is named for an ancient Viking interrogation practice, where you are strapped to a board while gravy-soaked meatballs are

LUTEFISK—THE MOST COLORFUL PART OF SCANDINAVIAN CULTURE

poured over your face until you confess that you're not hungry anymore.

AUSTRALIAN FOOD

Okay. Fine. You got me. Australian food isn't the *worst*. In fact, I'm a pretty big fan of their regional specialties, like the Bloomin' Onion, or the more exotic $19.99 New York Strip Steak.

A DINGO ATE MY BABY BACK RIBS!

FOOD AND POLITICS— IT'S THE GASTRONOMY, STUPID!

Separating American politics from food is like separating Americans from food: impossible. That's why every four years, presidential candidates gorge themselves on local delicacies. As the political theory goes, you are what you eat, so if I eat what you eat, then I'm you. Vote for you!

Average Americans want their political leaders to be able to stomach the same rendered scrapmeat they eat, which is often part stomach. Everybody knows the public votes for the guy they'd want to have a beer with, but we often forget that they're drinking that beer to wash the taste of Philly Cheez Whiz out of their mouths.

This gastro-gauntlet is how we weed out the candidates who aren't fit for office. Back in 2004, John Kerry suffered a setback when he ordered Swiss cheese on his cheesesteak. And more recently, Rick Santorum refused to put a Chicago hot dog in his mouth until the wiener had married the bun.

Turn the page for a map showing what you'll need to eat while you're waddling for President.

"LIKE YOU LOCALS, I TAKE PLEASURE FROM THE BREADED STICK MEAT"

EATING YOUR WAY TO COMMANDER-IN-BEEF

Seattle, WA:
Single cup of coffee, nursed for 9 hours in an independent coffee shop/bookstore/performance art/poetry slam laundromat

Portland, OR:
Artisinal meat loaf, Lo-fi potatoes, Apple pie that will *never* sell out

Montana:
Meat, Sky

North Dakota:
Dust, Wind, Hydrofracking chemicals. There is no food here.

Idaho:
Potato salad, Potato casserole, Potatoed potatoes

I don't know what state this is.

San Francisco, CA:
Rice-A-Roni, Rice-A-Pelosi, Rice-And-Two-Guys-Named-Tony

Las Vegas, NV:
Comped drinks, All-You-Can-Weep Despair Buffet

Utah:
Decaffeinated water

Colorado:
Rocky Mountain Oysters (bull testicles), Rocky Mountain Testicles (oysters)

Los Angeles, CA:
Sprig of parsley in saltwater reduction sauce and half-a-slow-roasted caper. Look! Tim Allen's at the next table! ($540)

Phoenix, AZ:
Tex-fully-documented-Mex

New Mexico:
Peyote buttons (required to secure endorsement of Coyote Spirit Governor)

Texas:
Last Meal leftovers

Alaska:
Salmon, King Crab, Previous statements criticizing oil industry

Hawaii:
Poi, Recently exhumed pig

Minnesota:
Cup of Mayonnaise

Wisconsin:
Life-size cheese sculpture of your head

Detroit, MI:
My Dust!

Chicago, IL:
Deep-Dish Pizza, Deeper-Dish Pizza, 20,000 Leagues Under the Cheese

Indiana:
White bread between two slices of white toast

Ohio:
Burger, fries, and Coke, Morbidly Biggied

Kentucky:
Filet of Bourbon

Tennessee:
Prettiest picture on menu

Mississippi:
Mud Pie, Dirt Quiche, Topsoil Tart

Alabama:
Heartrendingly Po' boys

Georgia:
Deep-fried something

New Orleans, LA:
Crawfish, Gumbo, Palpable post-Katrina resentment

New Hampshire:
Granite: Nature's Broom

Vermont:
Ben & Jerry's Pun-based Desserts, Antique doorknobs

New York:
Ray's Original Ray's Pizza of Ray's — Est. 2009

Pennsylvania:
Philly cheesesteak, Scrapple, Battery thrown by Eagles fan

West Virginia:
Dead canary

North Carolina:
BBQ

South Carolina:
BBQ, but good

Maine:
Lobster, 2 Gallons of Drawn Butter

Massachusetts:
Gay clam

Rhode Island:
You will not go to Rhode Island.

Connecticut:
Connecticutlets

New Jersey:
Saltwater taffy, Whatever slips by Chris Christie

Baltimore, MD:
Crab cakes, Crack cakes

District of Columbia:
100% all-taint hot dog. Because D.C. t'aint a state.

Delaware:
E4 from Rest Stop Vending Machine

Virginia:
Virginia ham, Virginia Slims

Cape Canaveral, FL:
Tang

Fort Lauderdale, FL:
Poon-Tang, am I right?

Miami, FL:
3-year-old Werther's Originals, Coconut shrimp, Cocaine shrimp

RN

NE

EASY
SOLUTIONS

fig 27.3-D. **STEPHEN COLBERT**

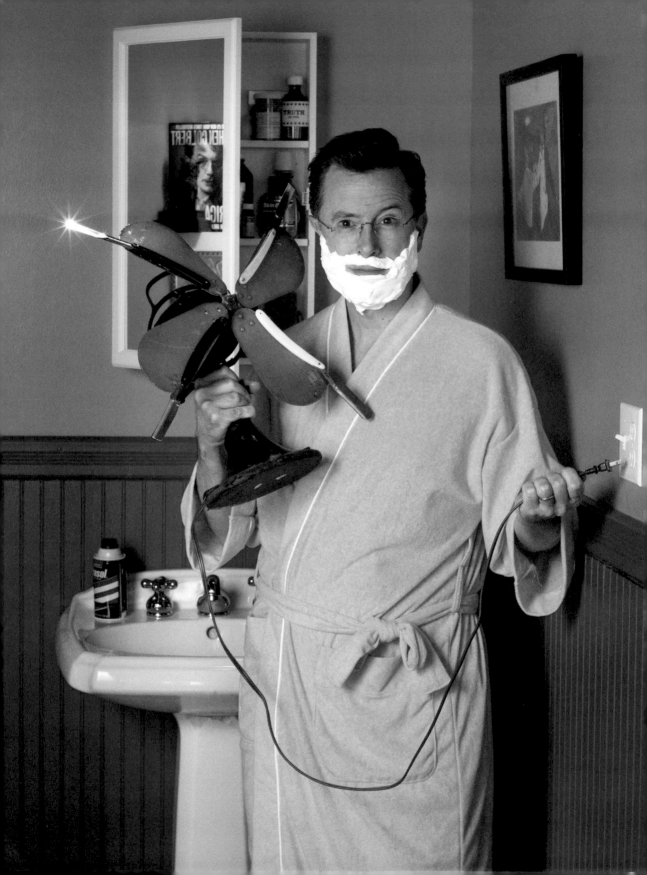

CHAPTER NINE

EASY SOLUTIONS

"FINDING AN APPROPRIATE QUOTATION FOR THIS
CHAPTER WAS REALLY HARD, SO I MADE ONE UP."
—René Descartes

Congratulations! You've almost made it to the end of the book. Pat yourself on the back! Actually, pat yourself on the eyes—they did most of the work.[1] I know you're sad that it's almost over; I feel the same depression when I'm on the last bite of a hoagie. Then I remember, I ordered a second hoagie! Then I get depressed again at the end of *that* hoagie, because why didn't I order a third hoagie?! But, wow, what a hoagie this book has been: we laughed, we cried, we fell asleep during the Federal Reserve part.

This book was my attempt to move America forward to re-become what it once was and never lost, again. It was about repairing a broken, perfect, shattered, flawless nation. We face tremendous challenges, but we can surmount these insurmountable mounts if we all work together. But when it comes to issues like our national debt, our long-term unemployment, and finding America's place in an increasingly global economy, we can all agree that there are no easy solutions.

---

[1] Don't forget to close them first.

But in case I'm wrong, here are some Easy Solutions.

★ Tax cuts.

★ Retrace our steps. Think about where we saw our thriving economy last. What jacket were we wearing?

★ Put on a show! If it worked for every Muppet movie, it can work to save America! I can twirl a baton and armpit-play "Bad, Bad Leroy Brown."

★ House flipping, but for states. We spruce up one of our clunkers—say, Indiana. Put in some new windows around Bloomington, lay down some rat traps around the Tippecanoe Battlefield. Then sell it off to some Saudi prince.

★ Let's get married. Look, I was thinking about it, and maybe we should just take the plunge. It'll get us out of our slump. And I'm sure once we're hitched, all our problems will just disappear, and not get more exaggerated over time.

★ Put it all on boxcars.

COME ON—DADDY NEEDS A NEW
INTERSTATE HIGHWAY SYSTEM!

★ Everybody get a fresh new haircut. That'll make us feel like a new country!

★ Check the couch cushions.

★ Bring the entire country to the Genius bar.

DON'T TELL HIM WE GOT AMERICA WET!

★ Raise the retirement age to "Decomposition."

★ Enforce a maximum 15-minute maternity leave.

★ Innovation. We need a new invention that will inspire us all and fill America with hope for a better tomorrow. I'm thinking a new Doritos flavor, something like Chedderggedon or Ranchgasm.

★ Change Children's Television Workshop to Children's Television Sweatshop.

★ Mandatory daily screenings of *Hotel Rwanda*. You'll quit complaining about $5 bank fees and start counting your blessings, such as the fingers you're counting them on.

★ Cutting taxes.

★ Open some good old-fashioned lemonade stands. And by "lemonade" I mean prostitution.

★ No minimum wage.

★ Pneumatic tubes. Everywhere.

★ Up Up Down Down Left Right Left Right B A B A Start.

★ Add "Under God" to every single line of the Pledge of Allegiance.

★ Flip to the back of the Constitution to see if it has the answers.

★ Eat a gallon of gelato and watch *The Bridges of Madison County*.

★ Powerball. Each of us buys 1 ticket. We split the winnings and give them to America.

★ I was watching *Ocean's Eleven* on USA, and I got a great heist idea. Let's rob the cast of *Ocean's Eleven*!

★ More surveillance cameras.

★ New currency: the bacon dollar. It's genius. It's never worthless, because you can always eat it. Though, we may need to invent some kind of raccoon-proof wallet.

★ Ooh, I know! Tax cuts!

★ Legalize it! For too long "it" has been illegal. Whatever "it" is, I have no clue, but people keep demanding "it" be legalized. And while we're at it, also legalize "that," and legalize "those."

★ One more *Rocky* film.

★ Hold down Texas, Maine and Oregon at the same time for a hard restart.

★ Take six months off to focus on our music.

★ Cut the red wire.

★ No, the blue wire!

★ Buy a Camaro and start diplomatic relations with a country half America's age.

★ Wait for our national debt to show up on Groupon at a massive discount.

★ Hold a 5K benefit walk to cure America.

★ Sing the National Anthem *twice* before football games.

★ Find a priceless Rembrandt at a garage sale.

★ Beetlejuice! Beetlejuice! Beetlejuice!

★ I know! Everyone get in the shower. That's where the best ideas happen.

★ Okay, I'm writing this one from the shower. So far, no America solutions but I did come up with an amazing screenplay idea: *Horny Toad*, the story of a frog with a crippling sex addiction. Call me, Pixar.

★ Use computers to fix it.

★ The encuttifying of our taxular system.

LEAVE IT FOR OUR GRANDCHILDREN. THEY'LL FIGURE IT OUT.

GOOD LUCK, SALLY!

I AM DRUNK

fig 28.3-D. **STEPHEN COLBERT**

★ **CHAPTER TEN** ★

I AM DRUNK

"I'M NOT DRUNK. **YOU'RE** *DRUNK!"*
—Stephen Colbert

I am drunk. And I earned it. I'm done! I did it! I fixed America again, which again, did not need fixing. And I'm gonna sit here and drink until my Pulitzer shows up. Started the night singing over at Lucky Chang's, but I guess there's a *limit* to how many times you can sing "America the Beautiful" in America! That number is 23, by the way. You don't see me going over to China and telling them to stop singing "Kung Fu Fighting." Whatever. Their loss. I'm feeling good.

Pistachio shells are so durable—you'd think they'd do something with them, like flooring—need thick shoes to walk on it, though.

Where was I? Right…finishing the book. Is the tape recorder on? Yes, it is. OK. The End!

America is great, and it *is* great.

So fuck Chang! Me and Tapey here have moved on to a classic American bar—Joe's Tavern. Dollar drafts, dartboards, Beer Nuts, hookah service, pita bread—'cause technically it's not "Joe's," it's "Yerfi's," and he's Turkish, but he plays enough Bon Jovi to make up for it. I love this place. In fact,

Statue of Lib:
w/ Big Boobs.
©colbert 2012

DEATH TO MY 000 FACE

← NO TIE

HOT DOG FIGHTING
MAHMOUD AHMADINEJAD

bartender, I'd like to buy a drink for everybody in this establishment! Then I'd like you to give them all to me.

AWWWOOOOOOOOOOOOOOOO! WEREWOLVES OF LONDON. AWWOOOOOOOO OOOOOOOOOOOO! SAW A WEREWOLF WITH A CHINESE MENU IN HIS HAND. WALKIN' THROUGH THE STREETS OF THE SOHO PLACE. AWOOOOOOOOOO OOOOOOOOOOOOOO. WEREWOLVES... No, YOU get down from the bar!

Fine. Guess it's just you and me, barstool. I wonder how far I can rock back on ya?

Hya, girl! Look at me, assholes! I'm Paul Revere! The British are coming! The British are—

I'm okay! I'm okay. Get off me, you filthy redcoats. Come on up, Stooly. You look thirsty. Could I get a bottle of ice and a bucket of cinnamon Schnapps?

This country is just getting so glonky. That's a word, right? Yeah, glonky. That's a total word.

Glonky, glonky, glonkyglonky-glonky. It's weird, you say it enough times, it starts to lose all glonky.

Have you seen China lately? That place is huge...and math.

Face it, we're *Rome*. The

Empire is crumbling at the edges. We live in the last decadent days of a dying giant, who's just trying to get in one last gay orgy before he falls on his samurai sword.

APPLE PIE W/
BIG BOOBS
©Colbert 2012

You ever wonder what it would be like to be gay? Not really gay, just like a gay Freaky Friday where me and a gay switch until we understand each other. Freaky FriGay. But none of the gay stuff that would *definitely* happen while I was gay— cuz c'mon, who would gay guys go for? Me or a gay guy—none of it would count once we switched back. That is the bedrock of freaky lifeswap.

God, I wish Jamie Lee Curtis was still alive.

And now, America's over. Roll credits: Executive Producer, George Washington. Based on the book *The Constitution*, by Sapphire.

WHOA

The barbarians are at the gates, and I bet you TURKS are first in line, licking your chops—what's Constantinople this time, Yerfi? New York? Los Angeles? Orlando? Space Mountain would make a hell of a mosque! It's a joke! C'mere, Yerf. Come here and let me hug you, you big furry Ottoman…

I'm just sad, okay? Just let me be sad.

God, I wish John Madden was still alive.

You don't get it! I have a responsibility with this book to hold the line against… wait, you stopped pouring rum into that glass. Keep pouring rum into that glass. Thank you.

Stoplight w/ Big Boobs.

© colbert 2012

So let's all raise a glass, and toast Ronald Reagan and Abraham Lincoln, riding horses together in Heaven. No, wait—it's Heaven. A tandem horse. Bottoms up!

Ow ow ow ow ow! Jesus, why are your candles in the exact same glasses as your drinks? Could I get some ice? And sterilize it with some rum.

Hey, look, some JOKER left his tape recorder on the bar! I'm going to leave a message on it. Hello, jerk, you left your tape recorder on the bar! You dummy! This is what you sound like: "Blah blah, tape recorder, I'm so important!" Ha… oh, man, that's good. I should be getting this down. Where's my tape recorder… HAS ANYONE SEEN MY TAPE RECORDER? IT LOOKS JUST LIKE THIS ONE! Forget it, I'll just use this one. Snooze you lose, dickburger! It's mine now! Barkeep, a pint of lager for my new friend the tape recorder here.

Okay, okay. You don't have to yell. I was leaving anyway. Right after I take a nap in this Pop-A-Shot machine. Hey! Nobody do Pop-A-Shot for a while, it's my bed now.

Ahhh. That's good.

I have a confession to make. I think about me all the time. I guess everybody does. But here's what I don't understand…everyone else's *me* is *them*! They're their own me! I'm only *my* me! If I care about America, do I have to care about all those other me's too? Oh shit! There's a "me" in "America." And an Erica!

INVENTIONS

① *PUT BAGELS ON A PIZZA SO YOU CAN HAVE BAGELS ANYTIME*

② *THE NECK HAT*

Ow! I said no Pop-A-Shot!

I'm so tired.

I'm so sorry.

Goodnight, America.

I love you.

And me.

And Erica.

MY BOOK w/ Big BOOBS

237

ACKNOWLEDGEMENTS

Thanks to Jamie Raab and her team at Grand Central Publishing: Bob Castillo, Toni Marotta, Eric Rayman, Siri Silleck, Flamur Tonuzi, Sara Weiss, and Tom Whatley. You guys published us real good.

An immense thank you to Stephen Doyle, Staci MacKenzie, Ben Tousley and the entire design team at Doyle Partners for being great and integral partners in the creation of this book. I'm embarrassed to tell you how many of the ideas were theirs.

Thanks to everyone for making the 3-D photos come alive: Andrew Matheson for his great eye and shutter speed; Brendan Hurley for the wonderful set designs; Antonia Xereas and Kerrie Plant-Price for making me look good; Jeremy Tchaban, Scott Heatherly and Ed Costello for the heavy lifting; as well as Mike Scricca and his team for lighting the way.

Thank you to Meredith Bennett for making this book a reality. Please stop us from doing this again.

Thanks to Michele Ganeless, Doug Herzog, Comedy Central, and everyone at the Viacom family of networks under the firm but fair leadership of Philippe Daumann who, I am not ashamed to say, I look to as a father figure.

Thank you to friends of the show Michael Lewis and Tim Meadows. You guys did things I'll never forget.

Thanks to Jon Stewart for being a great role model, James Dixon for making it happen, and Amy Cole for making *me* happen.

Thanks to the entire staff and crew of *The Colbert Report* tele-visual program—brought to you nightly in VistaVision—but especially Andro Buneta, Nate Charny, Megan Gearheart, Paul Hildebrand, Matt Lappin, Kristopher Long, Bill Marko, and Erica Myrickes for pulling double duty.

Thank you to the following people for your help in making the impossible possible:

Robert, Ryan, and Colin LaForty; Camille March and Henry Brumm; Jennifer, Luka, Aidan, and Mila Buneta; Leyla, Madison, Keira, and Zachary Dahm; Danielle St. Laurent and Giancarlo Dinello; Anne Martin, the Drysdales, and the Drydales; Cailin Goldberg-Meehan and the Dubbin family; Michele, Alex, and Chloe; the Gutermans and Haberles; Emily Gwinn Hall, Emmett and Oliver Gwinn; Carie, Jack, Tom and Hunter Hildebrand; Jennifer Kierans, Sean Julien, and Dexter; Adina, the Golds, Katsirs, Brookses & Lemeshows; Brian Lesser and Lois Gruhin Lesser; Sharon and Matthew Long; Katie Marko, the Marko and Feeney families; Rebecca Matheson; Popop Moreschi, Granny Shattuck, and Your Name Here; Andrew Sansone and the Scardino family; Rebecca, Beryl, and Leigh Sherman; the Werner family, Ali and the twins.

Thanks to Lorna Tuck and her hysterical brood. And thanks to Evie, Madeleine, Peter, and John. The book is done—I'm coming home.

If we missed anybody, please accept our apologies. We'll see you in the paperback. And if we miss you there, we'll see you in the neural brainwave implant ($26.99).

ORIGINAL ILLUSTRATIONS, GRAPHICS AND MOCKUPS:
Andro Buneta
Paul Hildebrand
Tim Hucklesby
Kristopher Long
Bill Marko
Rhoan O'Connell
Ali Qadeer
Karishma Sheth
Ben Tousley

ORIGINAL PHOTOGRAPHS BY:
Matt Lappin
Kristopher Long
Andrew Matheson

PHOTOS/ILLUSTRATIONS/ GRAPHICS/MOCKUPS:
Cover Photography:
Andrew Matheson
Hair: Katherine Drazens
Wardrobe Stylist: Antonia Xereas
Digital Imaging: Doyle Partners

CHAPTER 1 AMERICAN EXCEPTIONALISM Chapter opener: Matheson, Doyle Partners; American flag illustration: Tetra Images/ Getty, Marko; America pie chart illustration: James Brey/ Getty, Long; Newt Gingrich: Ethan Miller/Getty; America great exceptional diagram: Long, Doyle Partners; Kevin James and Leah Remini: AP; Ronald Reagan: Getty; Stalin moustache: Getty; slaves in the field*: Getty; Foot Soldiers photo mockup: Getty, Corbis, Buneta

CHAPTER 2 JOBS Chapter Opener: Matheson; Earie Canal illustration: Brian Evans/Getty, Long; unit sales target ratios chart: Long; jobless numbers math: Marko; President Barack Obama: Official White House Photo by Pete Souza; okie in the field*: Archive Holdings Inc/Getty; Rosie the Riveter: Getty; Beyonce: Wire Image/Getty; pizza chef illustration: Hildebrand; kama sutra illustration: Hildebrand; James Brown: Getty; virtuous buckle: Long; button: Long; snap: Long; velro: Long; zipper: Long; truth punch: Buneta; Lex Luthor: *SUPERMAN: The Movie* © Warner Bros. Entertainment Inc. All Rights Reserved; Luther Vandross: Wire Image/Getty; Martin Luther: Imagno/Getty; Martin Luther King Jr.: Library of Congress, Prints & Photographs Division, NYWT&S Collection, [reproduction number LC-USZ62-126559]; Lex Luthor King Jr. photo mockup: Library of Congress, Prints & Photographs Division, NYWT&S

Collection, [reproduction number LC-USZ62-126559], Marko; Greek attic red-figure plate: Ashmolean Museum, Oxford; Ayn Rand: © Oscar White/Corbis; Alan Greenspan photo mockup: Corbis, Long; house on fire: Bill Stormont/ Getty; Aynt and Grasshopper illustration: Buneta, Hildebrand; Samuel Gompers: Getty; Jim Belushi: Wire Image/Getty; Bobo mockup: Getty, Buneta; bowling alley attendant*: Marko, Long; Metallica illustration: Long; Stephen T. Colbert letterhead: Doyle Partners; Frat Grandpa photo mockup: Corbis, Getty, Hildebrand, Buneta; family portrait*: Digital Vision/Getty; shoe graph: Long; hair illustration: Long; Nigerian Prince Grandpa photo mockup: Corbis, Getty, Marko; handshake illustrations: Buneta; man with name tag*: Greg Seo/Getty, Buneta; man in bushes mockup*: Getty, Buneta; My Turn: Tim Hucklesby; unemployed Stephen*: Long, Buneta; Judge Judy: Getty

CHAPTER 3 HEALTHCARE
Chapter opener: Matheson; snow leopard with teeth: Joseph Van Os/Getty; Indian Woman*: Boris Breuer/Getty; Nicolas Cage: Getty; John Travolta: Wire Image/Getty; tobacco ad mockup*: Getty, Buneta; x-ray snow globe mockup: Getty, Buneta; Trojan Magnum condoms: Church & Dwight Co., Inc; horse: Digital Vision/Getty; colon license mockup: Getty, Marko; filibuster photo mockup*: Corbis, Getty, Hildebrand, Long; puppy: Stan Fellerman/Getty; chicken: Captain Vindaloo/Wikimedia Commons; baby Hitler photo mockup: Getty, Marko; Canadian Stephen photo mockup*: Getty, Marko; Doug McKenzie*: Norman Seeff Productions; doctor's office photo mockup: Getty, Hildebrand, Long; Queen Elizabeth II: AP; Moose: Tom Walker/Getty; Honey Nut Cheerios: Long; colorblind test mockup: Getty, Buneta, Hildebrand, Marko; skulls: Mittermeir/Getty; banana: Long; timberwolf: James Gritz/ Getty; Viagra pill 3D model: Hildebrand; man in blue shirt*: Siri Stafford/Getty; pill bottle: Long; promotional pens mockup: Getty, Buneta, Hildebrand; The Flying Nun: © Bettmann/Corbis; Burt Reynolds photo mockup: Corbis, Buneta; people bathing in the sunset photo mockup*: Getty, Hildebrand, Buneta; old couple*: Lucy Lambriex/Getty; waterfall:

Digital Vision/Getty; waterfall: Steve Casimiro/Getty; waterfall: Altus Photo Design/Getty; trees: Peter Adams/Getty; Airborne: Long; Nexium capsule: Lessin Leonard/Getty; multicolored pills: Long; Prescott Pharmaceuticals logo: Buneta; 10 sided die: Long; smoking lady photo mockup*: Corbis, Hildebrand; woman nasal cleansing*: Valery Rizzo/ Getty; ear candling*: Schultheiss Selection GmbH & CoKG/Getty; chiropractor visit*: Mel Yates/ Getty; crystal healing: Alan Levenson/Getty; glass ot water: Aaron Amat/ Shutterstock; meth: US Drug Enforcement Agency; spiders: Public-Domain-Image.com, Vicki Nunn & Ajor933/Wikimedia Commons, Buneta, Marko; suspicious mole illustration: Long; veterinarian*: GK Hart/Vikki Hart/Getty; laughing couple: CSA Images/Getty; mouse: AP; James Carville photo mockup: Corbis, Hildebrand, Marko; dachshund: Gary S. Chapman/ Getty, Marko; spinal subwoofer photo mockup*: Buneta; "What Your Doctor Isn't Telling You" book cover: Buneta, Hildebrand

CHAPTER 4 WALL STREET
Chapter opener: Matheson; Mr. Potter: Liberty Pictures; slot machine: Stephen Marks/Getty; Darth Vader at NYSE: Getty; distressed trader*: © Justin Guariglia/Corbis; prostitute*: AP; Alexander Hamilton portrait: John Trumbull/Wikimedia Commons; protesters with blank signs: Digital Vision/Getty; waiter photo mockup*: Corbis, Buneta; dominatrix*: Tricia Helfer from the film *Walk All Over Me*; swollen with health illustration: Meredith Scardino; investment banker*: © Bob Jacobson/Corbis; Zeus illustration: Buneta; Mr. Brenton Blankfien illustration: Marko; Mr. Lloyd Kunnelthorpe: Marko; Mr. Brenoyd Kunnelfein: Marko; grease stain: Buneta; water stain: Buneta; Rick Santelli: Getty; homeless man*: Thinkstock/Getty; Wall Street: Siegfried Layda/Getty; Michael Moore: AFP/Getty; Tamagachi: Long; paperclip: Buneta, Long; stock sail chart: Nanex, LLC; Jim Cramer photo mockup: AP, Buneta; man in green shirt*: Tatyana Chaiko/ Shutterstock; nurse and baby*: George Marks/Getty; backpacker*: Digital Vision/ Getty; Official Portrait of President Ronald Reagan by Executive Office of the President of the United States; buttoning jeans*: Peter Dazeley/Getty; $5

in pants: Hildebrand; men in top hats*: Hulton Collection/Getty; exterior NYSE: Keith Brofsky/ Getty; man with head in hands*: Kurt Hutton/Getty; shoes: Alfred Eisenstaedt/Getty; little boy*: Fairfax Media via Getty; Ernest Hemingway: Getty; Iwo Jima Statue: Vic Bider/Getty; kissing in Times Square: AP; Elvis: Time & Life Pictures/Getty; Michael J Fox: © CinemaPhoto/ Corbis; husband and wife*: Getty; Disney Monorail: © Neil Rabinowitz/Corbis; 60's woman*: SuperStock/Getty; marijuana leaf: AP; Woodstock poster: PR Newswire/AP; Nixon: AP; Gerald Ford: David Hume Kennerly, White House; Rocky: Getty; Jimmy Carter: Time & Life Pictures/Getty; cocaine: Long; man covering face*: Darren Robb/Getty; Rubik's cube: Long; man with hands on face*: Patti McConville/Getty; blackened catfish: Long; Sylvester Stallone: Getty; Friends: AP; OJ SImpson: AFP/Getty; computer: Long; Natalie Merchant: © Jon Ragel/Corbis; Milano: Long; Pets.com: Getty; Pets.com photo mockup: Getty, Long, Buneta; The Secret: Long; foreclosure: Fuse/Getty; hand signals*: Lappin, Marko; Bagger Vance: Getty; gardener photo mockup*: Getty, Marko; day trader Stephen photo mockup: Getty, Buneta, Long; woman on headset*: Shanna Baker/Getty; bake Sale: Angela Wyant/Getty; grandma*: Colin Anderson/Getty; recipe card chef illustration: Buneta; Federal Reserve Building: Hildebrand; Golden Girls: ABC Photo Archives/©ABC/Getty Images; Stephen holding Emmy®: Long; Hernando Cortez: Getty; gold nugget: ICHIRO/Getty; Gold chart: Marko; warrior photo mockup*: Getty, Hildebrand; Gold4Gold ad*: Comedy Partners, Getty, Buneta

CHAPTER 5 ENERGY Chapter opener: Matheson; blonde woman*: Mark Fairy / ©123RF; blonde woman on map mockup*: Mark Fairy/©123RF, Marko; mother and child at playground*: Bruce Ando/Getty; man with glasses*: Fotosearch/Getty; man in white hardhat*: Tyler Stableford/Getty; baby*: LWA/Getty; family with groceries: JGI/Tom Grill/Getty; man in suit*: Martin Barraud/ Getty; blonde woman photo mockup*: Mark Fairy/©123RF, Buneta; job checkbox: Buneta; campfire kids*: L. TITUS/Getty; oil rig: Simon Butterworth/

Getty; Eiffel Tower: **Kscolan/ Wikimedia Commons;** pelican in TV photo mockup: **AP, Marko;** oil: © Dragana **Jokmanovic/ iStockphoto;** smug deer: **Graham Langlands;** kids with stockings*: **Chris Ryan/Getty;** coal: **Lauren Burke/Getty;** Stephen holding coffee: **Lappin, Buneta;** man at computer*: **A J James/ Getty;** Picasso Guernica Painting: © The Gallery Collection/Corbis; pull my finger mockup*: **Brad Collett/Shutterstock, Lappin, Marko;** Evel Knieval: **Getty;** T-Frax skateboarding illustration: **Buneta;** cooling system: **Lappin;** T-Frax grandma illustration: **Buneta;** T-Frax tickling the earth illustration: **Buneta;** flame sink mockup: **Buneta;** dragon face illustration: **Hildebrand;** T-Frax farting illustration: **Buneta;** icy beard*: **Joe Henderson;** man camp: **AP;** South Dakota ad mockup: **Getty, United States Government, Buneta;** werewolf mockup*: **Getty, Hildebrand, Buneta;** sky: Medio images/Photodisc/Getty; mole man mockup*: **Universal Pictures Company Inc, Marko;** girl kissing a tree*: **ZenShui/ Antoine Arraou/Getty;** CO2 knob: **Buneta;** incandescent: **Marko;** fluorescent photo mockup*: **Lucasfilm/Paramount Pictures, Marko;** pelican photo mockup: **AP, Buneta**

CHAPTER 6 ELECTIONS
Chapter opener: **Matheson, Empire State Railway Museum;** Chris Matthews: **Frank Micelotta/PictureGroup via AP;** 30 Rock: **NBCUniversal;** Newt Gingrich: **AFP/Getty;** Rielle Hunter: © Patrick McMullan. com; Herman Cain: **Official Presidential campaign photo;** man playing the accordion*: © Brian Davis/Getty; e-mail boxes: **Buneta;** donate now illustration: **Buneta;** gum stick: **Buneta;** Mitt Romney: **Getty;** Goofy fight club photo mockup*: **Long, Buneta;** Supreme Court Justices: **Steve Petteway & Collection of the Supreme Court of the United States;** Supreme Court building: **Library of Congress, Prints & Photographs Division, Carol M. Highsmith Archive, [reproduction number LC-HS503-628];** Supreme Court Justice headshots for Roberts, Thomas, Scalia, Alito, and Kennedy: **Steve Petteway, Collection of the Supreme Court of the United States;** Supreme Court Justice Kennedy: **Robin Reid, Collection of the Supreme Court of the United States;** Super PACs! illustration: **Buneta;**

Super PAC Coordination Safety Guide illustration: **Marko;** "Daisy Girl" ad: **Screen grab from 1964 Johnson vs. Goldwater "Daisy Girl" commercial, as seen in "The Living Candidate," an online exhibition of the American Museum of the Moving Image. Courtesy of the American Museum of the Moving Image.;** "Willie Horton" ad: **Screen grab from 1988 Bush commercial. "Willie Horton," from "The Living Room Candidate," an online exhibition of the American Museum of the Moving image. Courtesy of the American Museum of the Moving Image.;** Let's All Go to the Lobby: **Filmack Studios;** old couple*: **Donna Day/ Getty;** *The Catcher in the Rye*: Little, Brown, and Company; *Pride And Prejudice*: **T. Egerton, Whitehall;** *Curious George*: Houghton Mifflin; *A Farewell To Arms*: **Scribner's;** *James and the Giant Peach*: **Puffin Books/ Scholastic;** *The Ugly Duckling*: **Morrow Junior Books;** *Adventures of Huckleberry Finn*: **Nelson Doubleday, Inc.;** *Winnie the Pooh*: **Dutton Children's Books;** Sarah Palin: **Getty;** Putin: **AP;** tandoori chicken: **Lappin;** Hitler button mockup: **Getty, Marko;** Moshe Dayan: **AP;** *Fantasia* Barino: **AP;** polling place*: **Hill Street Studios/Getty;** Twinkie: **Long;** young adult male*: **SergiyN/Shutterstock;** Mrs. Doubtfire: Twentieth Century Fox; Robin Williams: © Catherine Cabrol/Kipa/Corbis; blue collar Stephen photo mockup*: **Getty, Long**

CHAPTER 7 JUSTICE
Chapter opener: **Matheson;** Jorker illustration: **Long;** Stephen Cousteau photo mockup: **AP, Marko;** N.W.A. album mockup: **Priority Records, Marko;** cops rearview mirror: **Scott Richardson/Shutterstock;** PK Winsome*: **Long, Marko;** party animal registration*: **Long, Hildebrand;** Lake Minatare Lighthouse: **Brenda Leisy & James Hanna, Scotts Bluff County Tourism;** truck: **AP;** pumpkin: **DimiTalen/Wikimedia Commons;** lawn signs photo mockup: **Marko, Buneta;** Bible gun: **Marko;** flame thrower*: **Frank Rossoto Stocktrek/ Getty;** Good cop/Bad cop: **Long, Marko, Hildebrand;** Constitution: **National Archives and Records Administration;** cop arresting man*: **Moodboard/Getty;** jury summons*: **P_Wei/iStockphoto;** bedazzled juror photo mockup*: **Corbis, Lappin, Marko;** lawyer ad benches mockup*: **Buneta;**

laughing cartoon: **CSA Images/ B&W Archive Collection/Getty;** light bulb: **Buneta;** guard tower: **David Madison/Getty;** goal weight photo mockup*: **Getty, Long;** Jell-O molds: **Lappin, Hildebrand;** prisoners*: **Long, Lappin, Buneta, Hildebrand;** Jew*: **Lappin, Buneta;** Atticus Finch photo mockup*: **AP, Long**

CHAPTER 8 FOOD
Chapter opener: **Matheson, Doyle Partners;** American Eagle Outfitters: **Getty;** pink shirt man*: **Gelpi/Shutterstock;** Alaska map: **Long;** Tyson Any'tizers: **Long;** Daniel Day Lewis: **Getty;** monkey on a latke photo mockup: **Getty, Buneta;** DiGiorno Pizza Wyngz: **Long;** Huggies: **Long;** tomato: **Herr Stahlhoefer/ Wikimedia Commons;** milk: **Long;** potato: **Long;** sugarcane: **David Prince/Getty;** Agricultural Research Service; Stride Shift: **Long;** Trident: **Long;** Matthew McConaughey: **Wirelmage/Getty;** Connecticut Senator Joe Lieberman Official Senate Portrait: **AP;** Steven Tyler: **Wirelmage/Getty;** Rachael Ray: **Wirelmage/Getty;** Stephen the Colbert Report photo: **Courtesy of Comedy Central ©2012;** "JULIE & JULIA" ©2009 Columbia Pictures Industries, Inc. All Rights Reserved Courtesy of Columbia Pictures; Morely Safer: **FilmMagic/Getty;** Guy Fieri: **Getty;** Adam Richman photo mockup*: **Getty, AP, Buneta;** jeans: **Gemenacom/ Shutterstock;** locavore photo mockup*: **Getty, Buneta, Long;** borscht: **Alena Hrbková /Getty;** haggis: **Pichunter/iStockphoto;** blood sausage: **Robynmac/ iStockphoto;** Sardinian casu marzu (cheese): **David McLain/ Getty;** Ellis Island photo mockup: **Getty, General Mills, Buneta;** Slim Jim: **Long;** General Tso's chicken: **Paul Poplis/Getty;** burrito: **Long;** Mexican taco salad: **Long;** tapas: **Batista Moon Studio/Getty;** Ethiopian food: **Tim E White/Getty;** terrorist chickpea mockup: **Buneta;** snail: **Dimitri Vervitsiotis/ Getty;** lutefisk: **Long;** Outback Steakhouse: **Bloomberg via Getty;** Mitt Romney: **Romney for President Press Secretary Andrea Saul;** fajitas: **Long;** parsley on plate: **Long;** Rice A Roni: **Long;** bull: **Catherine Ledner/Getty;** vending machine: **Larsen & Talbert/Getty;** hot dog: **Long;** Tang: **Long;** spring breaker*: **Yuri Arcurs/Getty;** Werthers: **Long;** Georgia fried food: **Laurie Vogt/Getty;** pig:

© Renee Comet Photography/ the food passionares/Corbis; potatoes: **Long;** deep dish pizza: **Anna Andres/Getty;** bread sandwich: **Long;** bourbon: **Long;** crawfish: **Gentl & Hyers/Getty;** lobster: **Julien Capmeil/Getty;** crack: **US Drug Enforcement Agency;** gay clam: **Long;** car: **Long;** mayonnaise: **Long;** mud pie: **Brian Hagiwara/Getty;** steaks: **Long;** deck of cards and cocktail: **Long;** New Jersey Governor Chris Christie: **AP;** peyote: **U.S. Fish and Wildlife Service/ Wikimedia Commons;** pizza slice: **Long;** North & South Carolina BBQ: **Long;** po-boy: **Long;** meat loaf: **Martin Jacobs/Getty;** Philly cheesesteak: **Long;** Waffle House: **Colin Healy;** electric chair: **Getty;** water: **Long;** Virginia Slims: **Long;** coffee cup: **Long;** canary: **Buneta;** cheese: **AP;** Corn Palace: © Joseph Sohm/Visions of America/Corbis

CHAPTER 9 EASY SOLUTIONS
Chapter opener: **Matheson;** craps table: © Lise Gagne/iStockphoto; Genius Bar*: **AP;** Doritos mockup: **Getty, Lappin, Marko;** map mockup: **Buneta, Marko;** computer: **Henry Wolf/Getty;** little girl*: **Jill Tindall/Getty**

CHAPTER 10 I AM DRUNK
Chapter opener: **Matheson;** Statue of Lib, hot dog fighting, apple pie, stoplight, inventions, and book illustrations: **Meredith Scardino;** text message: **Buneta;** whoa illustration: **Peter Gwinn**

* The person depicted is a model.

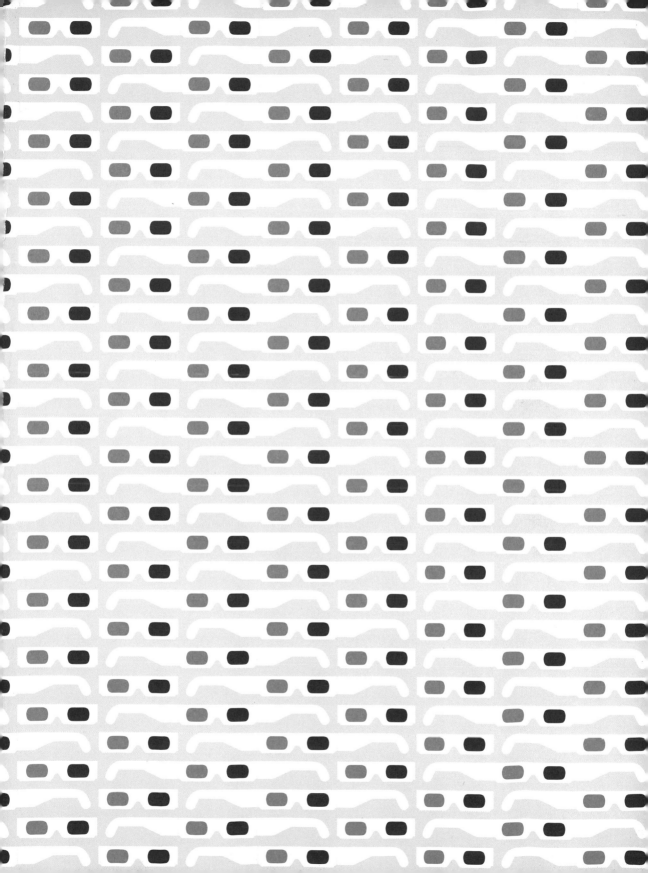

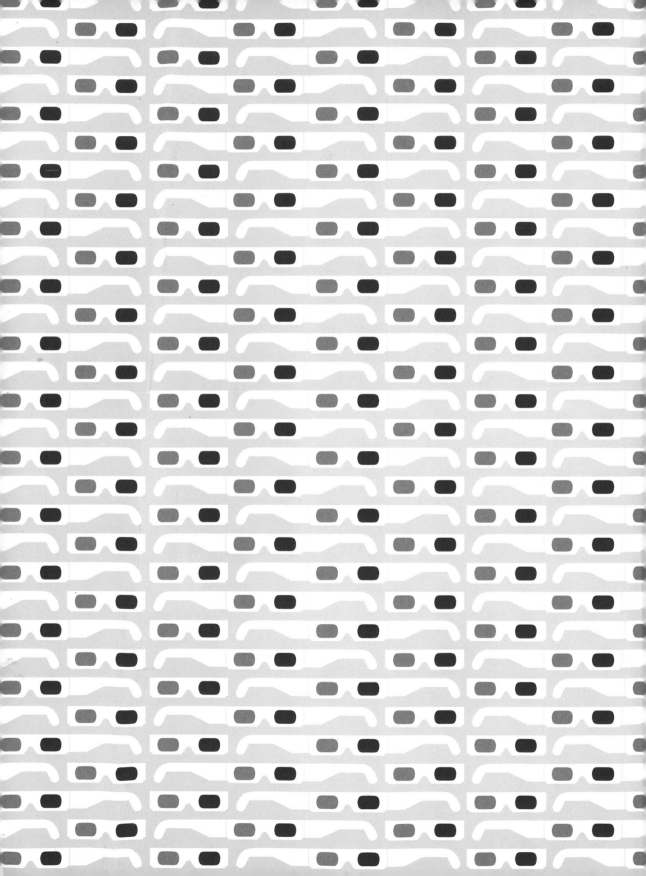